THE CONFESSIONS OF ST. AUGUSTINE

FOREWORD BY WARREN W. WIERSBE

BAKER BOOK HOUSE
Grand Rapids, Michigan

Reprinted 1977 by
Baker Book House

ISBN: 0-8010-0118-8

First printing, May 1977
Second printing, February 1980
Third printing, September 1981
Fourth printing, August 1984

PHOTOLITHOPRINTED BY CUSHING - MALLOY, INC.
ANN ARBOR, MICHIGAN, UNITED STATES OF AMERICA

FOREWORD

NO matter who you are, or what your religious experience may be, *The Confessions of St. Augustine* is a book that will help you.

The Confessions is probably the greatest autobiography ever written. To begin with, it is a very human book. It was written by a man whom we call a "saint," and yet he called himself a sinner! Augustine candidly tells us about his disappointments and failures, his search for truth, his sins, and then his meeting with God. He shares the pain of his restless, empty heart, and then he shares the joys of a heart filled with God. "Thou madest us for Thyself, and our heart is restless, until it repose in Thee," he writes.

But *The Confessions* is a book to stretch your mind as well as enrich your soul. Some have called *The Confessions* one of the greatest books of philosophy ever written. Augustine was not only a sinner who sought (and found) a Savior; he was also a thinker searching for ultimate truths. Augustine wrestles with questions such as: What is time? How is time related to eternity? How do we know God? How can we know anything?

Augustine was not afraid to tell God his doubts! Nor was he afraid to exercise his God-given intellect by confronting these difficult questions. If you want no part of the anti-intellectual, hyper-emotional brands of religious faith that are so common today, then read this book. It will teach you how to love God with all your mind as well as all your heart.

Augustine did not divorce the heart and the mind; he united them in his worship of God. For *The Confessions* is not only a book for seekers and doubters; it is also a book for worshipers. *The Confessions* is not addressed to the reader: it is addressed to God. The writer permits us to listen in as he worships God. We hear the deepest cries of confession as well as the highest expressions of praise. How we need a revival of personal and corporate worship today! I am convinced that this is the greatest need in our churches today. Too many Christians are living on substitutes and, sad to say, do not know the difference. If you desire to deepen your experience of worship, this book can help you.

When he first became a Christian, Augustine tried to separate himself from the world by joining a monastic society. However, providential circumstances forced him to change his plans. God called him back into the world that he might minister to the world. Courageously he opposed those who tried to bring false doctrine into the church. Faithfully he preached the Word to the great crowds that looked to him for spiritual food and guidance. *The Confessions,* unlike some other books of spiritual counsel, does not encourage Christians to escape from the world. Instead, the saintly bishop encourages us to get closer to God that we might be able to face the world. He invites us to the kind of spiritual experience Isaiah had in the temple when he "saw the Lord, high and lifted up!" Having seen the Lord, the prophet then saw himself and confessed his sins. It was then that God privileged him to see the needs of his world, and Isaiah left the temple to serve God and the people.

Augustine wrote this book at a time like ours, when everything stable seemed to be falling apart. The Roman Empire was crumbling, old customs and values were vanishing, strange new doctrines were appearing. The Christian Church was going through a turbulent time of transition and seemed to be losing its hold on society. Young people were rebellious and older people were frightened. Skepticism and outright atheism were popular.

How did Augustine respond to this challenge? *He looked to God!* He entered into a deeper relationship with Him. Then He translated his worship into service and went out to minister to the people.

It is not necessary to agree with all of Augustine's theology to benefit from the record of his experience. But *The Confessions* can be a deeply inspiring book if you will open your heart and mind to the truths that are in it. Read it carefully, meditatively; take time to think; take time to pray. Augustine surely intended his readers to set his book aside and lovingly worship the God he wrote about. "Seek the Lord," he writes, "and your soul shall live!"

WARREN W. WIERSBE

Important Dates

November 13, 354 — Augustine is born at Thagaste.

371-374 — Augustine is a student at Carthage.

375 — Augustine teaches at Thagaste.

376-383 — Augustine teaches at Carthage.

384 — Augustine goes to Milan and comes under the preaching of Ambrose.

August, 386 — Augustine is converted. He is baptized April 24, 387.

August, 388 — Augustine returns to Thagaste and gives himself to study.

391 — Augustine visits Hippo where the Bishop ordains him.

397 — Augustine becomes Bishop of Hippo. He writes *The Confessions* 397-400.

August 28, 430 — Augustine dies.

PREFACE

AMONG the companionable books that one might look for on a bedroom shelf, it is not everyone who would think of *The Confessions of St. Augustine*. They point to a kind of " angel knowledge " (to use Biron's word in *Love's Labour's Lost*), which most of us are afraid to take into our confidence. But then we must remember there are two Augustines : one the Saint haloed and magnified to the last dimension; the other, the man who in spite of the centuries and the accretions of his fame is a fellow-creature with ourselves. And of all his books, the *Confessions* lies nearest our sympathies, faced as we are by a predicament very like his own —confused by our fears and desires, and by that notional frenzy of which he complained among his acquaintances. As he in Rome or some Algerian town of his day, so we in our crowded place and time, are drawn many ways by many things—*in multis per multa*, as he says : and turn to him as a companion in misfortune, who went through with it, and at last found peace for his soul :

O let the Light, the Truth, the Light of my heart, not mine own darkness, speak unto me. I fell off into that and became darkened ; but even thence, even thence I loved Thee. I went astray, and remembered Thee. *I heard Thy voice behind me,* calling to me to return, and scarcely heard it, through the tumultuousness of the enemies of peace. And now, behold, I return in distress and panting after Thy fountain. Let no man forbid me! of this will I drink, and so live. Let me not be mine own life; from myself I lived ill, death was I to myself; and I revive in Thee. Do Thou speak unto me, do Thou discourse unto me. I have believed Thy books, and their words be most full of mystery.

Here, all that has been done is to let him tell in brief his own story, or so much of it as two ordinary readers who were familiar with it felt to be most suited to a plain man's bedroom companion. It puts into simpler form the quest of his " creaturely spirit," to quote one of his French critics, and provokes the reader to a fuller knowledge of " the great human-hearted penitent, the son of Monnica's tears, whose interest, like that of all great souls, is not of one century, but of all."

One of those Arab proverbs upon which he seems to draw at times, says : " Our town is but small; we must all know one another." This saying recalls at a glimpse what the village life and the Arab surroundings were amid which he grew up. Page after page of his own fills in the details of a life like our own under the foreign names of his native place and country. For he has the familiarising power; and Tagaste and Hippo, remote and antique though they are, affect us, by half-remembered associations, like landmarks we knew in another childhood.

PREFACE

At Tagaste—now named Souk Arras—some fifty miles inland from the Algerian coast, he was born. He was of African, probably of Berber blood;—and out of the likeness given him by Botticelli in the pillar of the church at Florence, and other fainter traces, we shape the imaginary figure of what the young Augustine may have been. We follow him to Madaura, a hot-blooded student; and so to Carthage; and our sense of that turbulent city—an outpost of the Romans against the African terror and the revolt of his own race, with all the vices of a mixed population, slaves and sybarites—Carthage, "the cesspool" as he terms it—is curiously altered as we relate it to his own spiritual history. There it was, in his twentieth year, he read Cicero's *Hortensius*, an exhortation to the study of philosophy. We engage with him deeply in his struggles—through philosophy less than divine, through astrology, through Manicheeism, and Donatism, through the lusts and the ailments of the flesh, and the snares of the schools —towards the large and simple divinity he sought.

The men and things that counted to him, the Faust of the subtle heresy, the friends about him —Alypius, "that clave to me by a most strong tie," faithful in little, faithful in much; Nebridius, most kind, most gentle ; and the master of his wisdom, that Ambrose whom Monnica loved as an angel—he makes them count to us by that kindling life-giving touch of his; that all-loving heart and mind, which made him one of the Great

Companions of all time. We see his circles of intimates as our own—see Alypius coming from his lawyer's office and Monnica carrying the basket, and hear the boy's voice chanting the call to the Book, " Take up and read! " which was Augustine's sign from Heaven.

The close community shown in the relations of Augustine and his group is a forecast in little of his whole idea of the Divine Communion; that idea, implicit in the *Confessions*, is worked out to its full dimensions in *The City of God*, which though not a book for a bedward man, is one to dwell upon in these times when the state seems to grow more and more secular and the City of Friends to lie farther and farther away.

But it is not *The City of God*, foundation-book as it is of a Christian civilisation that transcends our broken world, or the great doctrinal works of St. Augustine, which the modern reader will expect to find in this miniature of his mind. If we are to add anything now to this Golden Enchiridion, by way of grace, let it be a brief abstract from his *Soliloquies*. And first the page that tells in what humble state and contented poverty he went to Hippo:

I came to this city to see a friend whom I thought to win to God . . . they laid hands upon me and made me a priest ; and so it was I came in time to be a bishop. I brought nothing with me, and came to this See having only the clothes which I wore. . . . Valerian gave me the garden in which the convent now stands; and so I began to collect about me men of good will—possessing nothing as I had possessed nothing—that we might live a community life.

If you go on pilgrimage there to-day, you find no Hippo left to explore. The Carthaginian Ubbo, it became the Roman Hippo, or Hippone, and that in time was cut down into Bone. The modern town there is too French to remind one of the ancient city whose name it recalls; within half an hour's walk of its streets sixty years ago, a traveller spoke of the massive ruins of the immense water-cisterns and the scattered fragments of a few crumbling walls: more recently Mr. Belloc found scarcely a trace left of the lost city. But one likes to rebuild a ruined city, and to people a region again; and one goes in fancy to the valley of Augustine and restores the garden that Valerian gave, under the gaze of the bronze statue that recalls the good bishop on the hill. And thinking of the " City of God " he planned, we wonder at the rise and fall of the cities he knew: Carthage, Rome, Hippo. The year after his death, A.D. 430, the Vandals fell upon Hippo.

Add a few lines, a short colloquy between Augustine and his Reason on prayer:

A. I have prayed.
R. What then do you wish to know?
A. The things that I have prayed for.
R. Tell me them briefly.
A. God and the Soul.
R. Nothing more?
A. Nothing whatever.

SAINT AUGUSTINE

One cannot do better than complete that reduction to its elements of Augustine's piety and tireless search for illumination by one short prayer from the same source:

O God, our Father, listen to me groping amid these shadows, and stretch out to me Thy right hand. Hold Thy Light before me. Call me back from wandering Under Thy guidance, let me return to myself, let me return to Thee! AMEN.[1]

It remains to add a word to the reader about the illumination given to the text in this Golden Book by the footnotes. They will often be found to be the candles that make the gold visible.

E. R.

[1] From the version of St. Augustine's *Soliloquies* by Rose Elizabeth Cleveland.

CONTENTS

THE GOLDEN BOOK OF SAINT AUGUSTINE

CONFESSION OF THE GREATNESS OF GOD

*G*REAT *art Thou, O Lord, and greatly to be praised; great is Thy power, and Thy wisdom infinite.* And Thee would man praise; man, but a particle of Thy creation; man, that bears about him his mortality, the witness of his sin, the witness, that *Thou resistest the proud*: yet would man praise Thee; he, but a particle of Thy creation. Thou awakest us to delight in Thy praise; for Thou madest us for Thyself, and our heart is restless, until it repose in Thee. Grant me, Lord, to know and understand which is first, to call on Thee or to praise Thee? and, again, to know Thee or to call on Thee? For who can call on Thee, not knowing Thee? For he that knoweth thee not, may call on Thee as other than Thou art. Or, is it rather, that we call on Thee that we may know Thee? But *how shall they call on Him in whom they have not believed? or how shall they believe without a preacher?* And *they that seek the Lord shall*

1

praise Him. For *they that seek shall find Him,* and they that find shall praise Him. I will seek Thee, Lord, by calling on Thee; and will call on Thee, believing in Thee; for to us hast Thou been preached. My faith, Lord, shall call on Thee, which Thou hast given me, wherewith Thou hast inspired me, through the Incarnation of Thy Son, through the ministry of the Preacher.[1]

* * *

For who is Lord but the Lord? or who is God save our God? Most highest, most good, most potent, most omnipotent; most merciful, yet most just; most hidden, yet most present; most beautiful, yet most strong; stable, yet incomprehensible; unchangeable, yet all-changing; never new, never old; all-renewing, and *bringing age upon the proud, and they know it not*; ever working, ever at rest; still gathering, yet nothing lacking; supporting, filling, and overspreading; creating, nourishing, and maturing; seeking, yet having all things. Thou lovest, without passion; art jealous, without anxiety; repentest, yet grievest not; art angry, yet serene; changest Thy words, Thy purpose unchanged; receivest again what Thou findest, yet didst never lose; never in need, yet rejoicing in gains; never covetous, yet exacting usury. Thou receivest over and above, that Thou mayest owe; and who hath aught that is not Thine? Thou payest debts,

---

[1] St. Ambrose; from whom were the beginnings of his conversion, and by whom he was baptised.

owing nothing; remittest debts, losing nothing. And what have I now said, my God, my life, my holy joy? or what saith any man when he speaks of Thee? Yet woe to him that speaketh not, since mute are even the most eloquent.

Oh! that I might repose on Thee! Oh! that Thou wouldest enter into my heart, and inebriate it, that I may forget my ills, and embrace Thee, my sole good! What art Thou to me? In Thy pity, teach me to utter it. Or what am I to Thee that Thou demandest my love, and, if I give it not, art wroth with me, and threatenest me with grievous woes? Is it then a slight woe to love Thee not? Oh! for Thy mercies' sake, tell me, O Lord my God, what Thou art unto me. *Say unto my soul, I am thy salvation.* So speak, that I may hear. Behold, Lord, my heart is before Thee; open Thou the ears thereof, and *say unto my soul, I am thy salvation.* After this voice let me haste, and take hold on Thee. Hide not Thy face from me. Let me die—lest I die—only let me see Thy face.

INFANCY

NARROW is the mansion of my soul; enlarge Thou it, that Thou mayest enter in. It is ruinous; repair Thou it. It has that within which must offend Thine eyes; I confess and know it. But who shall cleanse it? or to whom should I cry, save Thee? *Lord, cleanse me from my secret faults, and spare Thy servant from the power of the enemy. I believe, and therefore do I speak.* Lord, Thou knowest. *Have I not confessed against myself my transgressions unto Thee, and Thou, my God, hast forgiven the iniquity of my heart?* I contend not in judgment with Thee, who art the truth; I fear to deceive myself; *lest mine iniquity lie unto itself.* Therefore I contend not in judgment with Thee; *for if Thou, Lord, shouldest mark iniquities, O Lord, who shall abide it?*

Yet suffer me to speak unto Thy mercy, me, *dust and ashes.* Yet suffer me to speak, since I speak to Thy mercy, and not to scornful man. Thou too, perhaps, despisest me, yet wilt Thou *return and have compassion* upon me. For what would I say, O Lord my God, but that I know not whence I came into this dying life (shall I call it?) or living death. Then immediately did the comforts of Thy compassion take me up, as I heard (for I remember it not) from the parents of my flesh, out of whose substance Thou didst some-time fashion me. Thus there received me the comforts of woman's milk. For neither my mother nor my nurses stored their own breasts for me; but Thou didst bestow the food of my infancy through them, according to Thine ordinance, whereby Thou distributest Thy riches through the hidden springs of all things. Thou also gavest me to desire no more than Thou gavest; and to my nurses willingly to give me what Thou gavest them. For they, with an heaven-taught affection, willingly gave me what they abounded with from Thee. For this my good from them, was good for them. Nor, indeed, from them was it, but through them; for from Thee, O God, are all good things, and *from my God is all my health*. This I since learned, Thou, through these Thy gifts, within me and without, proclaiming Thyself unto me. For then I knew but to suck; to repose in what pleased, and cry at what offended my flesh; nothing more.

Afterwards I began to smile; first in sleep, then waking: for so it was told me of myself, and I believed it; for we see the like in other infants, though of myself I remember it not. Thus, little by little, I became conscious where I was; and to have a wish to express my wishes to those who could content them, and I could not; for the wishes were within me, and they without; nor could they by any sense of theirs enter within my spirit. So I flung about at random limbs and voice, making the few signs I could, and such as I could, like, though in truth very little like, what I wished. And when I was not presently obeyed (my wishes being hurtful or unintelligible), then I was indignant with my elders for not submitting to me, with those owing me no service, for not serving me; and avenged myself on them by tears. Such have I learnt infants to be from observing them; and, that I was myself such, they, all unconscious, have shown me better than my nurses who knew it.

And, lo! my infancy died long since, and I live. But Thou, Lord, who for ever livest, and in whom nothing dies: for before the foundation of the worlds, and before all that can be called "before," Thou art, and art God and Lord of all which Thou hast created: in Thee abide, fixed for ever, the first causes of all things unabiding; and of all things changeable, the springs abide in Thee unchangeable: and in Thee live the eternal reasons of all things unreasoning and temporal. Say, Lord, to me, Thy suppliant; say, all-pitying, to me, Thy pitiable one; say, did my infancy succeed another age of mine that died before it? Was it that which I spent within my mother's womb? for of that I have heard somewhat, and have myself seen women with child; and what before that life again, O God my joy, was I any where or any body? For this have I none to tell me, neither father nor mother, nor experience of others, nor mine own memory. Dost Thou mock me for asking this, and bid me praise Thee and acknowledge Thee, for that I do know?

INFANCY

I acknowledge Thee, Lord of heaven and earth, and praise Thee for my first rudiments of being, and my infancy, whereof I remember nothing; for Thou hast appointed that man should from others guess much as to himself; and believe much on the strength of weak females. Even then I had being and life, and (at my infancy's close) I could seek for signs, whereby to make known to others my sensations. Whence could such a being be, save from Thee, Lord? Shall any be his own artificer? Or can there elsewhere be derived any vein, which may stream essence and life into us, save from Thee, O Lord, in whom essence and life are one? for Thou Thyself art supremely Essence and Life. *For Thou art most high, and art not changed,* neither in Thee doth To-day come to a close; yet in Thee doth it come to a close; because all such things also are in Thee. For they had no way to pass away, unless Thou upheldest them. And since *Thy years fail not,* Thy years are one To-day. How many of ours and our fathers' years have flowed away through Thy " to-day," and from it received the measure and the mould of such being as they had; and still others shall flow away, and so receive the mould of their degree of being. But *Thou art still the same,* and all things of to-morrow, and all beyond, and all of yesterday, and all behind it, Thou hast done to-day.

MONNICA: HIS MOTHER'S CARE

AS a boy I had already heard of an eternal life, promised us through the humility of the Lord our God stooping to our pride; and even from the womb of my mother, who greatly hoped in Thee, I was sealed with the mark of His cross and salted with His salt.[1] Thou sawest, Lord, how while yet a boy, being seized on a time with sudden oppression of the stomach, and like near to death—Thou sawest, my God (for Thou wert my keeper), with what eagerness and what faith I sought, from the pious care of my mother and Thy Church, the mother of us all, the baptism of Thy Christ my God and Lord. Whereupon the mother of my flesh, being much troubled (since, with a heart pure in Thy faith, she even more lovingly *travailed in birth* of my salvation), would in eager haste have provided for my consecration and cleansing by the health-giving sacraments, confessing Thee, Lord Jesus, for the remission of sins, unless I had suddenly recovered. And so, as if I must needs be again polluted should I live, my cleansing was deferred, because the defilements of sin would, after that washing, bring greater and more perilous

[1] A rite in the Western Churches, on admission as a catechumen, previous to baptism, denoting the purity and uncorruptedness required of Christians.

guilt. I then already believed; and my mother, and the whole household, except my father: yet did not he prevail over the power of my mother's piety in me, that as he did not yet believe, so neither should I. For it was her earnest care, that Thou my God, rather than he, shouldest be my father; and in this Thou didst aid her to prevail over her husband, whom she, the better, obeyed, therein also obeying Thee, who hast so commanded.

I beseech Thee, my God, I would fain know, if so Thou willest, for what purpose my baptism was then deferred? Was it for my good that the rein was laid loose, as it were, upon me, for me to sin? or was it not laid loose? If not, why does it still echo in our ears on all sides, " Let him alone, let him do as he will, for he is not yet baptised "? but as to bodily health, no one says, " Let him be worse wounded, for he is not yet healed." How much better then, had I been at once healed; and then, by my friends' diligence and my own, my soul's recovered health had been kept safe in Thy keeping who gavest it. Better truly. But how many and great waves of temptation seemed to hang over me after my boyhood! These my mother foresaw; and preferred to expose to them the clay whence I might afterwards be moulded, than the very cast, when made.[1]

* * *

[1] His unregenerate nature, on which the image of God was not yet impressed, rather than the regenerate.

This was the world at whose gate unhappy I lay in my boyhood; this the stage, where I had feared more to commit a barbarism, than having committed one, to envy those who had not. These things I speak and confess to Thee, my God; for which I had praise from them, whom I then thought it all virtue to please. For I saw not the abyss of vileness, wherein *I was cast away from Thine eyes.* Before them what more foul than I was already, displeasing even such as myself? with innumerable lies deceiving my tutor, my masters, my parents, from love of play, eagerness to see vain shows, and restlessness to imitate them! Thefts also I committed, from my parents' cellar and table, enslaved by greediness, or that I might have to give to boys, who sold me their play, which all the while they liked no less than I. In this play, too, I often sought unfair conquests, conquered myself meanwhile by vain desire of pre-eminence. And what could I so ill endure, or, when I detected it, upbraided I so fiercely, as that I was doing to others? and for which if, detected, I was upbraided, I chose rather to quarrel, than to yield. And is this the innocence of boyhood? Not so, Lord, not so; I cry Thy mercy, O my God. For these very sins, as riper years succeed, these very sins are transferred from tutors and masters, from nuts and balls and sparrows, to magistrates and kings, to gold and manors and slaves, just as severer punishments displace the cane. It was the low stature then of childhood, which Thou our King didst command as an emblem of lowliness, when Thou saidst, *Of such is the kingdom of heaven.*

Yet, Lord, to Thee, the Creator and Governor of the universe, most excellent and most good, thanks were due to Thee our God, even hadst Thou destined for me boyhood only. For even then I was, I lived, and felt; and had an implanted providence over my own well-being—a trace of that mysterious Unity,[1] whence I was derived;—I guarded by the inward sense the entireness of my senses, and in these minute pursuits, and in my thoughts on things minute, I learnt to delight in truth, I hated to be deceived, had a vigorous memory, was gifted with speech, and soothed by friendship, avoided pain, baseness, ignorance. In so small a creature, what was not wonderful, not admirable? But all are gifts of my God; it was not I, who gave them me; and good these are, and these together are myself. Good, then, is He that made me, and He is my good; and before Him will I exult for every good which of a boy I had. For it was my sin, that not in Him, but in His creatures—myself and others—I sought for pleasures, sublimities, truths, and so fell headlong into

---

[1] " To be, is no other than to be one. In as far, therefore, as anything attains unity, in so far it ' is.' For unity worketh congruity and harmony, whereby things composite are, in so far as they are: for things uncompounded are in themselves, because they are one; but things compounded, imitate unity by the harmony of their parts, and, so far as they attain to unity, they are. Wherefore order and rule secure being, disorder tends to not-being." Aug. de Morib. Manich. c. 6.

sorrows, confusions, errors. Thanks be to Thee, my joy and my glory and my confidence, my God, thanks be to Thee for Thy gifts; but do Thou preserve them to me. For so wilt Thou preserve me, and those things shall be enlarged and perfected, which Thou hast given me, and I myself shall be with Thee, since even to be Thou hast given me.

AT CARTHAGE

TO Carthage I came, where they sang all around me in my ears a cauldron of unholy loves. I loved not yet, yet I loved to love, and out of a deep-seated want, I hated myself for wanting not. I sought what I might love, in love with loving, and safety I hated, and a way without snares. For within me was a famine of that inward food, Thyself, my God; yet, through that famine I was not hungered; but was without all longing for incorruptible sustenance, not because filled therewith, but the more empty, the more I loathed it. For this cause my soul was sickly and full of sores, it miserably cast itself forth, desiring to be scraped by the touch of objects of sense. Yet if these had not a soul, they would not be objects of love. To love then, and to be beloved, was sweet to me; but more, when I obtained to enjoy the person I loved. I defiled, therefore, the spring of friendship with the filth of concupiscence, and I beclouded its brightness with the hell of lustfulness; and thus foul and unseemly, I would fain, through exceeding vanity, be fine and courtly. I fell headlong then into the love wherein I longed to be ensnared. My God, my Mercy, with how much gall didst Thou out of Thy great goodness besprinkle for me that sweetness? For I was both beloved, and secretly arrived at the bond of enjoying; and was with joy fettered with sorrow-bringing bonds, that I might be scourged with the iron burning rods of jealousy, and suspicions, and fears, and angers, and quarrels.

Stage-plays also carried me away, full of images of my miseries, and of fuel to my fire. Why is it, that man desires to be made sad, beholding doleful and tragical things, which yet himself would by no means suffer? yet he desires as a spectator to feel sorrow at them, and this very sorrow is his pleasure. What is this but a miserable madness? for a man is the more affected with these actions, the less free he is from such affections. Howsoever, when he suffers in his own person, it uses to be styled misery: when he compassionates others, then it is mercy. But what sort of compassion is this for feigned and scenical passions? for the auditor is not called on to relieve, but only to grieve: and he applauds the actor of these fictions the more, the more he grieves. And if the calamities of those persons (whether of old times, or mere fiction) be so acted, that the spectator is not moved to tears, he goes away disgusted and criticising; but if he be moved to passion, he stays intent, and weeps for joy.

Are griefs then too loved? Verily all desire joy. Or whereas no man likes to be miserable, is he yet pleased to be merciful? which because it cannot be without passion, for this reason alone are passions loved? This also springs from that vein of friendship. But whither goes that vein? whither flows it? wherefore runs it into that[1] torrent of pitch bubbling forth those monstrous tides of foul lustfulness, into which it is wilfully changed and transformed, being of its own will precipitated and corrupted from its heavenly clearness? Shall compassion then be put away? By no means. For griefs too be sometimes loved. But beware of uncleanness, O my soul, under the guardianship of my God, the *God of my fathers, who is to be praised and exalted above all for ever,* beware of uncleanness. For I have not now ceased to pity; but then in the theatres I rejoiced with lovers, when they wickedly enjoyed one another, although this was imaginary only in the play. And when they lost one another, as if very compassionate, I sorrowed with them, yet had my delight in both. But now I much more pity him that rejoiceth in his wickedness, than him who is thought to suffer hardship, by missing some pernicious pleasure, and the loss of some miserable felicity. This certainly is the truer mercy, but in it grief delights not. For though he that grieves for the miserable, be commended for his office of charity; yet had he, who is genuinely compassionate, rather there were nothing for him to grieve for. For if good will be ill willed (which can never be), then

[1] He alludes to the sea of Sodom, which is said to bubble out a pitchy slime, into which other rivers running, are there lost in it, and like the lake itself, remain unmovable: wherefore it is called the Dead Sea.

may he, who truly and sincerely commiserates, wish there might be some miserable, that he might commiserate. Some sorrow may then be allowed, none loved. For thus dost Thou, O Lord God, who lovest souls far more purely than we, and hast more incorruptibly pity on them, yet art wounded with no sorrowfulness. *And who is sufficient for these things?*

But I, miserable, then loved to grieve, and sought out what to grieve at, when in another's and that feigned and personated misery, that acting best pleased me, and attracted me the most vehemently, which drew tears from me. What marvel that an unhappy sheep, straying from Thy flock, and impatient of Thy keeping, I became infected with a foul disease? And hence the love of griefs; not such as should sink deep into me; for I loved not to suffer what I loved to look on; but such as upon hearing their fictions should lightly scratch the surface; upon which as on envenomed nails, followed inflamed swelling, impostumes, and a putrefied sore. My life being such, was it life, O my God?

And Thy faithful mercy hovered over me afar. Upon how grievous iniquities consumed I myself, pursuing a sacrilegious curiosity, that having forsaken Thee, it might bring me to the treacherous abyss, and the beguiling service of devils, to whom I sacrificed my evil actions, and in all these things Thou didst scourge me! I dared even, while Thy solemnities were celebrated within the walls of Thy

Church, to desire, and to compass a business, deserving death for its fruits, for which Thou scourgedst me with grievous punishments, though nothing to my fault, O Thou my exceeding mercy, my God, my refuge from those terrible destroyers, among whom I wandered with a stiff neck, withdrawing further from Thee, loving mine own ways, and not Thine; loving a vagrant liberty.

Those studies also, which were accounted commendable, had a view to excelling in the courts of litigation; the more bepraised, the craftier. Such is men's blindness, glorying even in their blindness. And now I was chief in the rhetoric school, whereat I joyed proudly, and I swelled with arrogancy, though (Lord, Thou knowest) far quieter and altogether removed from the subvertings of those " Subverters " [1] (for this ill-omened and devilish name was the very badge of gallantry) among whom I lived, with a shameless shame that I was not even as they. With them I lived, and was sometimes delighted with their friendship, whose doings I ever did abhor, i.e. their " subvertings," wherewith they wantonly persecuted the modesty of strangers, which they disturbed by a gratuitous jeering, feeding thereon their malicious mirth. Nothing can be liker the very actions of devils

[1] Eversores. This appears to have been a name which a pestilent and savage set of persons gave themselves, licentious alike in speech and action. Augustine names them again elsewhere, whence they seem to have consisted mainly of Carthaginian students, whose savage life is mentioned by him.

than these. What then could they be more truly called than " subverters " ? themselves subverted and altogether perverted first, the deceiving spirits secretly deriding and seducing them, wherein themselves delight to jeer at, and deceive others.

Among such as these, in that unsettled age of mine, learned I books of eloquence, wherein I desired to be eminent, out of a damnable and vainglorious end, a joy in human vanity. In the ordinary course of study, I fell upon a certain book of Cicero, whose speech almost all admire, not so his heart. This book of his contains an exhortation to philosophy, and is called *Hortensius*. But this book altered my affections, and turned my prayers to Thyself, O Lord; and made me have other purposes and desires. Every vain hope at once became worthless to me; and I longed with an incredibly burning desire for an immortality of wisdom, and began now to arise, that I might return to Thee. For not to sharpen my tongue (which thing I seemed to be purchasing with my mother's allowances, in that my nineteenth year, my father being dead two years before), not to sharpen my tongue did I employ that book; nor did it infuse into me its style, but its matter.

How did I burn then, my God, how did I burn to re-mount from earthly things to Thee, nor knew I what Thou wouldest do with me! For with Thee is wisdom. But the love of wisdom is in Greek called " philosophy," with which that book inflamed me. Some there be that seduce through philosophy, under a great, and smooth, and honourable name colouring and disguising their own errors: and almost all who in that and former ages were such, are in that book censured and set forth: there also is made plain that wholesome advice of Thy Spirit, by Thy good and devout servant: *Beware lest any man spoil you through philosophy and vain deceit, after the tradition of men, after the rudiments of the world, and not after Christ. For in Him dwelleth all the fulness of the Godhead bodily.* And since at that time (Thou, O light of my heart, knowest) Apostolic Scripture was not known to me, I was delighted with that exhortation, so far only, that I was thereby strongly roused, and kindled, and inflamed to love, and seek, and obtain, and hold, and embrace not this or that sect, but wisdom itself whatever it were; and this alone checked me thus enkindled, that the name of Christ was not in it. For this name, according to Thy mercy, O Lord, this name of my Saviour Thy Son, had my tender heart, even with my mother's milk, devoutly drunk in, and deeply treasured; and whatsoever was without that name, though never so learned, polished, or true, took not entire hold of me.

I resolved then to bend my mind to the holy Scriptures, that I might see what they were. But behold, I see a thing not understood by the proud, nor laid open to children, lowly in access, in its recesses lofty, and veiled with mysteries; and I was not such as could enter into it, or stoop my neck to follow its steps. For not as I now speak, did I feel when I turned to those Scriptures; but they seemed to me unworthy to be compared to the stateliness of Tully: for my swelling pride shrunk from their lowliness, nor could my sharp wit pierce the interior thereof. Yet were they such as would grow up in a little one. But I disdained to be a little one; and, swollen with pride, took myself to be a great one.

Therefore I fell among men proudly doting, exceeding carnal and prating, in whose mouths were the snares of the Devil, limed with the mixture of the syllables of Thy name, and of our Lord Jesus Christ, and of the Holy Ghost, the Paraclete, our Comforter. These names departed not out of their mouth, but so far forth, as the sound only and the noise of the tongue, for the heart was void of truth. Yet they cried out " Truth, Truth," and spake much thereof to me, yet *it was not in them*: but they spake falsehood, not of Thee only (who truly art Truth), but even of those elements of this world, Thy creatures. And I indeed ought to have passed by even philosophers who spake truth concerning them, for love of Thee, my Father, supremely good, Beauty of all things beautiful. O Truth, Truth, how inwardly did even then the marrow of my soul pant after Thee, when they often and diversely, and in many and huge books, echoed of Thee to me, though it was but an echo? And these were the dishes wherein to me, hungering after Thee, they, instead of Thee, served up the

Sun and Moon, beautiful works of Thine, but yet Thy works, not Thyself, no nor Thy first works.

For thy spiritual works are before these corporeal works, celestial though they be, and shining. But I hungered and thirsted not even after those first works of Thine, but after Thee Thyself, the Truth, *in whom is no variableness, neither shadow of turning*: yet they still set before me in those dishes, glittering fantasies, than which better were it to love this very sun (which is real to our sight at least), than those fantasies which by our eyes deceive our mind. Yet because I thought them to be Thee, I fed thereon; not eagerly, for Thou didst not in them taste to me as Thou art; for Thou wast not these emptinesses, nor was I nourished by them, but exhausted rather. Food in sleep shows very like our food awake; yet are not those asleep nourished by it, for they are asleep. But those were not even any way like to Thee, as Thou hast now spoken to me; for those were corporeal fantasies, false bodies, than which these true bodies, celestial or terrestrial, which with our fleshly sight we behold, are far more certain: these things the beasts and birds discern as well as we, and they are more certain than when we fancy them. And again, we do with more certainty fancy them, than by them conjecture other vaster and infinite bodies which have no being. Such empty husks was I then fed on; and was not fed. But Thou, my soul's Love, *in looking for whom I fail*, that I may become strong, art neither those bodies which we see, though in heaven; nor those which we see not there; for Thou hast created them, nor dost Thou account them among the chiefest of Thy works. How far then art Thou from those fantasies of mine, fantasies of bodies which altogether are not, than which the images of those bodies, which are, are far more certain, and more certain still the bodies themselves, which yet Thou art not; no, nor yet the soul, which is the life of the bodies. So then, better and more certain is the life of the bodies, than the bodies. But Thou art the life of souls, the life of lives, having life in Thyself; and changest not, life of my soul.

* * *

And Thou *sentest Thine hand from above*, and drewest my soul out of that profound darkness, my mother, Thy faithful one, weeping to Thee for me, more than mothers weep the bodily deaths of their children. For she, by that faith and spirit which she had from Thee, discerned the death wherein I lay, and Thou heardest her, O Lord; Thou heardest her, and despisedst not her tears, when streaming down, they watered the ground under her eyes in every place where she prayed; yea Thou heardest her. For whence was that dream whereby Thou comfortedst her; so that she allowed me to live with her, and to eat at the same table in the house, which she had begun to shrink from, abhorring and detesting the blasphemies of my error? For she saw herself standing on a certain wooden rule, and a shining youth coming towards her, cheerful and smiling upon her, herself grieving, and overwhelmed with grief. But he having (in order to instruct, as is their wont, not to be instructed) inquired of her the causes of her grief and daily tears, and she answering that she was bewailing my perdition, he bade her rest contented, and told her to look and observe, "That where she was, there was I also." And when she looked, she saw me standing by her in the same rule. Whence was this, but that Thine ears were towards her heart? O Thou Good omnipotent, who so carest for every one of us, as if Thou caredst for him only; and so for all, as if they were but one!

Whence was this also, that when she has told me this vision, and I would fain bend it to mean, "That she rather should not despair of being one day what I was"; she presently, without any hesitation, replies: "No; for it was not told me that, 'where he, there thou also'; but 'where thou, there he also'"? I confess to Thee, O Lord, that to the best of my remembrance (and I have oft spoken of this), that Thy answer, through my waking mother,—that she was not perplexed by the plausibility of my false interpretation and so quickly saw what was to be seen, and which I certainly had not perceived, before she spake,— even then moved me more than the dream itself, by which a joy to the holy woman, to be fulfilled so long after, was, for the consolation of her present anguish, so long before foresignified. For almost nine years passed, in which I wallowed in the mire of that deep pit, and the darkness of falsehood, often assaying to rise, but dashed down the more grievously. All which time that chaste, godly, and sober widow (such as Thou lovest), now more cheered with hope, yet no whit relaxing in her weeping and mourning, ceased not at all hours of her devotions to bewail my case to Thee. And her *prayers entered into Thy presence*; and yet Thou sufferest me to be yet involved and reinvolved in that darkness.

Thou gavest her meantime another answer, which I call to mind; for much I pass by, hasting to those things which more press me to confess unto Thee, and much I do not remember. Thou gavest her then another answer, by a Priest of Thine, a certain Bishop brought up in Thy Church, and well studied in Thy books. Whom when this woman had entreated to vouchsafe to converse with me, refute my errors, unteach me ill things, and teach me good things (for this he was wont to do, when he found persons fitted to receive it), he refused, wisely, as I afterwards perceived. For he answered, that I was yet unteachable, being puffed up with the novelty of that heresy, and had already perplexed divers unskilful persons with captious questions, as she had told him: " But let him alone a while " (saith he), " only pray God for him, he will of himself by reading find what that error is, and how great its impiety." At the same time he told her, how himself, when a little one, had by his seduced mother been consigned over to the Manichees, and had not only read, but frequently copied out almost all, their books, and had (without any argument or proof from any one) seen how much that sect was to be avoided; and had avoided it. Which when he had said, and she would not be satisfied, but urged him more, with entreaties and many tears, that he would see me, and discourse with me; he, a little displeased at her importunity, saith, "Go thy ways, and God bless thee, for it is not possible that the son of these tears should perish." Which answer she took (as she often mentioned in her conversations with me) as if it had sounded from heaven.

THE SACRIFICE OF THANKSGIVING

SUFFER me, I beseech Thee, O my God, and give me grace to go over in my present remembrance the wanderings of my forepassed time, and *to offer unto Thee the sacrifice of thanksgiving*. For what am I to myself without Thee, but a guide to mine own downfall;[1] or what am I even at the best, but an infant sucking the milk Thou givest, and feeding upon Thee, *the food that perisheth not?* But what sort of man is any man, seeing he is but a man?

* * *

There was in those days a wise man, very skilful in physic, and renowned therein, who had with his own proconsular hand put the Agonistic garland upon my distempered head, but not as a physician: for this disease Thou only curest, *who resistest the proud, and givest grace to the humble.*

[1] " To be happy, by his own power, without superintendence, belongs to God only." Aug. de Gen. c. Manich. ii. 5. " He alone is truly pure, who waiteth on God, and keepeth himself to Him alone." Aug. de Vita Beata, sec. 18. " Whoso seeketh God, is pure, because the soul hath in God her legitimate Husband. Whosoever seeketh of God any thing besides God, doth not love God purely. If a wife loveth her husband, because he is rich, she is not pure, for she loveth not her husband, but the gold of her husband." Aug. Serm. 137. " Whoso seeks from God any other reward but God, and for it would serve God, esteems what he wishes to receive, more than Him from whom he would receive it. What then? hath God no reward? None, save Himself. The reward of God is God Himself." Aug. in Ps. 72, sec. 32.

But didst Thou fail me even by that old man, or forbear to heal my soul? For having become more acquainted with him, and hanging assiduously and fixedly on his speech (for though in simple terms, it was vivid, lively, and earnest), when he had gathered by my discourse, that I was given to the books of nativity-casters, he kindly and fatherly advised me to cast them away, and not fruitlessly bestow a care and diligence, necessary for useful things, upon these vanities; saying, that he had in his earliest years studied that art, so as to make it the profession whereby he should live, and that, understanding Hippocrates, he could soon have understood such a study as this; and yet he had given it over, and taken to physic, for no other reason but that he found it utterly false; and he, a grave man, would not get his living by deluding people. " But thou," saith he, " hast rhetoric to maintain thyself by, so that thou followest this of free choice, not of necessity: the more then oughtest thou to give me credit herein, who laboured to acquire it so perfectly, as to get my living by it alone." Of whom when I had demanded, how then could many true things be foretold by it, he answered me (as he could) " that the force of chance, diffused throughout the whole order of things, brought this about. For if when a man by haphazard opens the pages of some poet, who sang and thought of something wholly different, a verse oftentimes fell out, wondrously agreeable to the present business: it were not to be wondered at, if out of the soul of man, unconscious what takes place in it, by some higher instinct an answer should be given, by hap, not by art, corresponding to the business and actions of the demander."

And thus much, either from or through him, Thou conveyedst to me, and tracedst in my memory, what I might hereafter examine for myself. But at that time neither he, nor my dearest Nebridius, a youth singularly good and of a holy fear, who derided the whole body of divination, could persuade me to cast it aside, the authority of the authors swaying me yet more, and as yet I had found no certain proof (such as I sought) whereby it might without all doubt appear, that what had been truly foretold by those consulted was the result of haphazard, not of the art of the star-gazers.

In those years when I first began to teach rhetoric in my native town, I had made one my friend, but too dear to me, from a community of pursuits, of mine own age, and, as myself, in the first opening flower of youth. He had grown up of a child with me, and we had been both school-fellows and play-fellows. But he was not yet my friend as afterwards, nor even then, as true friendship is; for true it cannot be, unless in such as Thou cementest together, cleaving unto Thee, by that *love which is shed abroad in our hearts by the Holy Ghost, which is given unto us*. Yet was it but too sweet, ripened by the warmth of kindred studies: for, from the true faith (which he as a youth had not soundly and thoroughly imbibed), I had warped him also to those superstitious and pernicious fables, for which my mother bewailed me. With me he now erred in mind, nor could my soul be without him. But behold Thou wert close on the steps of Thy fugitives, at once *God of vengeance*, and Fountain of mercies, turning us to Thyself by wonderful means; Thou tookest that man out of this life, when he had scarce filled up one whole year of my friendship, sweet to me above all sweetness of that my life.

Who can recount all Thy praises, which he hath felt in his one self? What diddest Thou then, my God, and how unsearchable is the *abyss of Thy judgments*? For long, sore sick of a fever, he lay senseless in a death-sweat; and his recovery being despaired of, he was baptised, unknowing; myself meanwhile little regarding, and presuming that his soul would retain rather what it had received of me, not what was wrought on his unconscious body. But it proved far otherwise: for he was refreshed, and restored. Forthwith, as soon as I could speak with him (and I could, so soon as he was able, for I never left him, and we hung but too much upon each other), I essayed to jest with him, as though he would jest with me at that baptism which he had received, when utterly absent in mind and feeling, but had now understood that he had received. But he so shrunk from me, as from an enemy; and with a wonderful and sudden freedom bade me, as I would continue his friend, forbear such language to him. I, all astonished and amazed, suppressed all my emotions till he should grow well, and his health were strong enough for me to deal with him, as I would. But he was taken away from my frenzy, that with Thee he might be preserved for my comfort; a few days after, in my absence, he was attacked again by the fever, and so departed.

At this grief my heart was utterly darkened; and whatever I beheld was death. My native country was a torment to me, and my father's house a strange unhappiness; and whatever I had shared with him, wanting him, became a distracting torture. Mine eyes sought him everywhere, but he was not granted them; and I hated all places, for that they had not him; nor could they now tell me, "he is coming," as when he was alive and absent. I became a great riddle to myself, and I asked my soul, *why she was so sad, and why she disquieted me sorely* : but she knew not what to answer me. And if I said, *Trust in God*, she very rightly obeyed me not; because that most dear friend, whom she had lost, was, being man, both truer and better than that phantasm she was bid to trust in. Only tears were sweet to me, for they succeeded my friend, in the dearest of my affections.

And now, Lord, these things are passed by, and time hath assuaged my wound. May I learn from Thee, who art Truth, and approach the ear of my heart unto Thy mouth, that Thou mayest tell me why weeping is sweet to the miserable? Hast Thou, although present everywhere, cast away our misery far from Thee? And Thou abidest in

Thyself, but we are tossed about in divers trials. And yet unless we mourned in Thine ears, we should have no hope left. Whence then is sweet fruit gathered from the bitterness of life, from groaning, tears, sighs, and complaints? Does this sweeten it, that we hope Thou hearest? This is true of prayer, for therein is a longing to approach unto Thee. But is it also in grief for a thing lost, and the sorrow wherewith I was then overwhelmed? For I neither hoped he should return to life, nor did I desire this with my tears; but I wept only and grieved. For I was miserable, and had lost my joy. Or is weeping indeed a bitter thing, and for very loathing of the things, which we before enjoyed, does it then, when we shrink from them, please us?

But what speak I of these things? for now is no time to question, but to confess unto Thee. Wretched I was; and wretched is every soul bound by the friendship of perishable things; he is torn asunder when he loses them, and then he feels the wretchedness which he had ere yet he lost them. So it was then with me; I wept most bitterly, and found my repose in bitterness. Thus was I wretched, and that wretched life I held dearer than my friend.[1] For though I would willingly have changed it, yet

[1] " Were any to say, I had rather die than be unhappy, I should answer, ' Thou speakest false.' For now thou art unhappy, and willest not to die, for no other cause than to be; so then, though you will not to be unhappy, you do will to be. Give thanks then for that thou art, which thou dost will, that so what thou art against thy will may be removed from thee. For willingly thou art, but unwillingly art unhappy." Aug. de Lib. Arb. iii. sec. 10.

was I more unwilling to part with it, than with him; yea, I know not whether I would have parted with it even for him, as is related (if not feigned) of Pylades and Orestes, that they would gladly have died for each other or together, not to live together being to them worse than death. But in me there had arisen some unexplained feeling, too contrary to this, for at once I loathed exceedingly to live, and feared to die. I suppose, the more I loved him, the more did I hate and fear (as a most cruel enemy) death, which had bereaved me of him: and I imagined it would speedily make an end of all men, since it had power over him. Thus it was with me, I remember. Behold my heart, O my God, behold and see into me; for well I remember it, O my Hope, who cleansest me from the impurity of such affections, directing *mine eyes towards Thee*, and *plucking my feet out of the snare*. For I wondered that others, subject to death, did live, since he whom I loved, as if he should never die, was dead: and I wondered yet more that myself, who was to him a second self, could live, he being dead. Well said one of his friend, " Thou half of my soul ": for I felt that my soul and his soul were " one soul in two bodies ": and therefore was my life a horror to me, because I would not live halved. And therefore perchance I feared to die, lest he whom I had much loved should die wholly.

O madness, which knowest not how to love men, like men! O foolish man that I then was, enduring impatiently the lot of man! I fretted then, sighed, wept, was distracted; had neither rest nor counsel. For I bore about a shattered and bleeding soul, impatient of being borne by me, yet where to repose it, I found not. Not in calm groves, nor in games and music, nor in fragrant spots, nor in curious banquetings, nor in the pleasures of the bed and the couch; nor (finally) in books or poesy, found it repose. All things looked ghastly, yea, the very light; whatsoever was not what he was, was revolting and hateful, except groaning and tears. For in those alone found I a little refreshment. But when my soul was withdrawn from them, a huge load of misery weighed me down. To Thee, O Lord, it ought to have been raised, for Thee to lighten; I knew it; but neither could nor would; the more, since, when I thought of Thee, Thou wert not to me any solid or substantial thing. For Thou wert not Thyself, but a mere phantom, and my error was my God. If I offered to discharge my load thereon, that it might rest, it glided through the void, and came rushing down again on me; and I had remained to myself a hapless spot, where I could neither be, nor be from thence. For whither should my heart flee from my heart? Whither should I flee from myself? Whither not follow myself? And yet I fled out of my country; for so should mine eyes less look for him, where they were not wont to see him. And thus from Tagaste I came to Carthage.

TIMES LOSE NO TIME

TIMES lose no time; nor do they roll idly by; through our senses they work strange operations on the mind. Behold, they went and came day by day, and by coming and going, introduced into my mind other imaginations, and other remembrances; and little by little patched me up again with my old kind of delights, unto which that my sorrow gave way. And yet there succeeded, not indeed other griefs, yet the causes of other griefs. For whence had that former grief so easily reached my very inmost soul, but that I had poured out my soul upon the dust, in loving one that must die, as if he would never die? For what restored and refreshed me chiefly, was the solaces of other friends, with whom I did love, what instead of Thee I loved: and this was a great fable, and protracted lie, by whose adulterous stimulus, our soul, which lay itching in our ears, was being defiled. But that fable would not die to me, so oft as any of my friends died. There were other things which in them did more take my mind; to talk and jest together, to do kind offices by turns; to read together honied books; to play the fool or be earnest together; to dissent at times without discontent, as a man might with his own self; and

34

even with the seldomness of these dissentings, to season our more frequent consentings; sometimes to teach, and sometimes learn; long for the absent with impatience; and welcome the coming with joy. These and the like expressions, proceeding out of the hearts of those that loved and were loved again, by the countenance, the tongue, the eyes, and a thousand pleasing gestures, were so much fuel to melt our souls together, and out of many make but one.

This is it that is loved in friends; and so loved, that a man's conscience condemns itself, if he love not him that loves him again, or love not again him that loves him, looking for nothing from his person but indications of his love. Hence that mourning, if one die, and darkenings of sorrows, that steeping of the heart in tears, all sweetness turned to bitterness; and upon the loss of life of the dying, the death of the living. Blessed whoso loveth Thee, and his friend in Thee, and his enemy for Thee. For he alone loses none dear to him, to whom all are dear in Him who cannot be lost. And who is this but our God, the *God that made heaven and earth*, and *filleth them*, because by filling them He created them? Thee none loseth, but who leaveth. And who leaveth Thee, whither goeth or whither fleeth he, but from Thee well-pleased, to Thee displeased? For where doth he not find Thy law in his own punishment? *And Thy law is truth*, and truth Thou.

Turn us, O God of Hosts, show us Thy countenance,

and we shall be whole. For whithersoever the soul of man turns itself, unless towards Thee, it is riveted upon sorrows, yea, though it is riveted on things beautiful. And yet they, out of Thee, and out of the soul, were not, unless they were from Thee. They rise, and set; and by rising, they begin as it were to be; they grow, that they may be perfected; and perfected, they wax old and wither; and all grow not old, but all wither. So then when they rise and tend to be, the more quickly they grow that they may be, so much the more they haste not to be. This is the law of them. Thus much hast Thou allotted them, because they are portions of things, which exist not all at once, but by passing away and succeeding, they together complete that universe, whereof they are portions. And even thus is our speech completed by signs giving forth a sound: but this again is not perfected unless one word pass away when it hath sounded its part, that another may succeed. Out of all these things let my soul praise Thee, O God, Creator of all; yet let not my soul be riveted unto these things with the glue of love, through the senses of the body. For they go whither they were to go, that they might not be; and they rend her with pestilent longings, because she longs to be, yet loves to repose in what she loves.[1] But in these things is no place of repose;

[1] " In this life men, with much toil, seek rest and freedom from care, but through perverse longings they find it not. They wish to find rest in things which rest and abide not, and these, since they are withdrawn by time and pass away,

36

they abide not, they flee; and who can follow them with the senses of the flesh? yea, who can grasp them when they are hard by? For the sense of the flesh is slow, because it is the sense of the flesh; and thereby is it bounded. It sufficeth for that it was made for; but it sufficeth not to stay things running their course from their appointed starting-place to the end appointed. For in Thy word, by which they are created, they hear their decree, "hence and hitherto."

Be not foolish, O my soul, nor become deaf in the ear of thine heart with the tumult of thy folly. Hearken thou too. The Word Itself calleth thee to return: and there is the place of rest imperturbable, where love is not forsaken, if itself forsaketh not. Behold, these things pass away, that others may replace them, and so this lower universe be completed by all his parts. But do I depart any whither? saith the Word of God. There fix thy dwelling, trust there whatsoever thou hast thence, O my soul, at least now thou art tired out with vanities. Entrust Truth, whatsoever thou hast from the Truth, and thou shalt lose nothing; and thy decay shall bloom again, and *all thy diseases be healed*, and thy mortal parts be re-formed and renewed, and bound around thee: nor shall they lay thee whither themselves descend; but they shall stand fast with thee, and abide for ever before God, *who abideth* and standeth fast *for ever*.

harass them with fears and sorrows, and will not let them be at rest." Aug. de Catechiz. Rud. sec. 14.

Why then be perverted and follow thy flesh? Be it converted and follow thee. Whatever by her thou hast sense of, is in part; and the whole, whereof these are parts, thou knowest not; and yet they delight thee. But had the sense of thy flesh a capacity for comprehending the whole, and not itself also, for thy punishment, been justly restricted to a part of the whole, thou wouldest, that whatsoever existeth at this present, should pass away, that so the whole might better please thee. For what we speak also, by the same sense of the flesh thou hearest; yet wouldest not thou have the syllables stay, but fly away, that others may come, and thou hear the whole. And so ever, when any one thing is made up of many, all of which do not exist together, all collectively would please more than they do severally, could all be perceived collectively. But far better than these, is He who made all; and He is our God, nor doth He pass away, for neither doth aught succeed Him.

If bodies please thee, praise God on occasion of them, and turn back thy love upon their Maker;[1]

---

[1] "Wherever you turn, He speaketh to thee by traces, which He has impressed upon His works, and by the very forms of outward things recalls thee, when sinking down to things outward.—Woe to them who leave Thee as their guide, and go astray in the traces of Thee, who, for Thee, love these intimations of Thee, and forget what Thou intimatest, O Wisdom, Thou most sweet light of the cleansed mind! for Thou ceasest not to intimate to us what and how great Thou art, and these intimations of Thee is the universal beauty of creation." Aug. de Lib. Arb. ii. 16.

lest in these things which please thee, thou displease. If souls please thee, be they loved in God: for they too are mutable, but in Him are they firmly stablished; else would they pass, and pass away. In Him then be they beloved; and carry unto Him along with thee what souls thou canst, and say to them, " Him let us love, Him let us love; He made these, nor is He far off. For He did not make them, and so depart, but they are of Him, and in Him. See there He is, where truth is loved. He is within the very heart, yet hath the heart strayed from Him. *Go back into your heart*,[1] *ye transgressors*, and cleave fast to Him that made you. Stand with Him, and ye shall stand fast. Rest in Him, and ye shall be at rest. Whither go ye in rough ways？ Whither go ye？ The good that you love is from Him;[2] but it is

---

[1] " Because men, seeking things without, become strange even to themselves, the written law also was given them; not because it was not already written in their hearts, but because thou wert strayed, as a vagabond, from thy own heart, so He, who is everywhere, laid hold on thee, and recalled thee to thine own inward self. What then does the written law cry aloud to such as have forsaken the law written in their hearts？ ' Return to your hearts, ye transgressors.'—What then thou wouldest not have done to thee, do not to another. Thou decidest it to be evil, in that thou wouldest not endure it, and the inward law, written in thy very heart, forces thee to know this. Thou didst it, and men groaned at thy hands; how art thou forced to ' go back into thy own heart,' when thou endurest it at the hands of others." Aug. in Ps. 57, sec. 1.

[2] " Shame we, since other things are only loved, as being good, by cleaving to them to cease to love Him, through whom they are good."

good and pleasant through reference to Him, and
justly shall it be embittered, because unjustly is
anything loved which is from Him, if He be forsaken for it. To what end then would ye still and
still walk these difficult and toilsome ways? There
is no rest, where ye seek it. Seek what ye seek;
but it is not there where ye seek. Ye seek a blessed
life in the land of death; it is not there. For
how should there be a blessed life, where life
itself is not?

"But our true Life came down hither, and bore
our death, and slew him, out of the abundance
of His own life; and He thundered, calling aloud
to us to return hence to Him into that secret place,
whence He came forth to us, first into the Virgin's
womb, wherein He espoused the human creation,
our mortal flesh, that it might not be for ever
mortal, and thence *like a bridegroom coming out
of his chamber, rejoicing as a giant to run his course.*
For He lingered not, but ran, calling aloud by
words, deeds, death, life, descent, ascension; crying aloud to us to return unto Him. And He departed from our eyes, that we might return into
our heart, and there find Him. For He departed,
and lo, He is here. He would not be long with us,
yet left us not; for He departed thither, whence
He never parted, *because the world was made by
Him.* And *in this world He was, and into this world
He came to save sinners,* unto whom my soul confesseth, *and He healeth it, for it hath sinned against
Him.* O ye sons of men, how long so slow of heart?

*Even now, after the descent of Life to you, will ye
not ascend and live ?* But whither ascend ye, when
ye are on high, and *set your mouth against the
heavens ?* Descend, that ye may ascend,[1] and ascend
to God. For ye have fallen, by ascending against
Him."[2] Tell them this, that they may weep *in
the valley of tears,* and so carry them up with thee
unto God; because not of His Spirit thou speakest
thus unto them, if thou speakest, burning with the
fire of charity.

These things I then knew not, and I loved these
lower beauties, and I was sinking to the very depths,
and to my friends I said, "Do we love anything
but the beautiful? What then is the beautiful?
and what is beauty? What is it that attracts and
wins us to the things we love? for unless there

---

[1] "It is a perverted loftiness, when men deserting that
whereto the mind should cleave as to its first principle,
would become and be, as it were, a first principle to itself.
—There is then, strange to say, something in humility,
which raises the heart upwards, and something in elation,
which sinks it downwards.—A reverent humility makes one
subject to him who is higher; but nothing is higher than
God; and so humility, which makes subject to God, exalts.
But a faulty elation, in that it rejects this subjection, sinks
down from Him, than whom nothing is higher, and thereby
becomes lower." Aug. de Civ. Dei, xiv. 13.

[2] "By the lowliness of repentance the soul recovers her
high estate." Aug. de Lib. Arb. iii. 5. "He made a way for us
through humility; because through pride we had departed
from God, we could not return but through humility, and
one to take as a pattern we had not. For the whole mortal
nature of man was swelled with pride.—Lest then men
should disdain to follow a humble man, God humbled Himself; that even the pride of the human race might not disdain
to follow the track of God." Aug. in Ps. 33. Enarr. l. sec. 4.

were in them a grace and beauty, they could by no means draw us unto them." And I marked and perceived that in bodies themselves, there was a beauty, from their forming a sort of whole, and again, another from apt and mutual correspondence, as of a part of the body with its whole, or a shoe with a foot, and the like. And this consideration sprang up in my mind, out of my inmost heart, and I wrote, " on the fair and fit," I think, two or three books. Thou knowest, O Lord, for it is gone from me; for I have them not, but they are strayed from me, I know not how.

But what moved me, O Lord my God, to dedicate these books unto Hierius, an orator of Rome, whom I knew not by face, but loved for the fame of his learning which was eminent in him, and some words of his I had heard, which pleased me? But more did he please me, for that he pleased others, who highly extolled him, amazed that out of a Syrian, first instructed in Greek eloquence, should afterwards be formed a wonderful Latin orator, and one most learned in things pertaining unto philosophy. One is commended, and, unseen, he is loved: doth this love enter the heart of the hearer from the mouth of the commender? Not so. But by one who loveth is another kindled. For hence he is loved, who is commended, when the commender is believed to extol him with an unfeigned heart; that is, when one that loves him, praises him.

For so did I then love men, upon the judgment

of men, not Thine, O my God, in whom no man is deceived. But yet why not for qualities, like those of a famous charioteer, or fighter with beasts in the theatre, known far and wide by a vulgar popularity, but far otherwise, and earnestly, and so as I would be myself commended? For I would not be commended or loved, as actors are (though I myself did commend and love them), but had rather be unknown, than so known; and even hated, than so loved. Where now are the impulses to such various and divers kinds of loves laid up in one soul? Why, since we are equally men, do I love in another what, if I did not hate, I should not spurn and cast from myself? For it holds not, that as a good horse is loved by him, who would not, though he might, be that horse, therefore the same may be said of an actor, who shares our nature. Do I then love in a man, what I hate to be, who am a man? *Man himself is a great deep, whose very hairs Thou numberest, O Lord, and they fall not to the ground without Thee.* And yet are the hairs of his head easier to be numbered, than are his feelings, and the beatings of his heart.

But that orator was of that sort whom I loved, as wishing to be myself such; and I erred through a swelling pride, and *was tossed about with every wind*, but yet was steered by Thee, though very secretly. And whence do I know, and whence do I confidently confess unto Thee, that I had loved him more for the love of his commenders, than for the very things for which he was commended?

Because, had he been unpraised, and these self-same men had dispraised him, and with dispraise and contempt told the very same things of him, I had never been so kindled and excited to love him. And yet the things had not been other, nor he himself other; but only the feelings of the relators. See where the impotent soul lies along, that is not yet stayed up by the solidity of truth!

*　　*　　*

I saw not yet, whereon this weighty matter turned in Thy wisdom, O Thou Omnipotent, *who only doest wonders*; and my mind ranged through corporeal forms; and " fair," I defined and distinguished what is so in itself, and " fit," whose beauty is in correspondence to some other thing: and this I supported by corporeal examples. And I turned to the nature of the mind, but the false notion which I had of spiritual things, let me not see the truth. Yet the force of truth did of itself flash into mine eyes, and I turned away my panting soul from incorporeal substance to lineaments, and colours, and bulky magnitudes. And not being able to see these in the mind, I thought I could not see my mind. And whereas in virtue I loved peace, and in viciousness I abhorred discord; in the first I observed an unity, but in the other, a sort of division. And in that unity, I conceived the rational soul, and the nature of truth and of the chief good to consist: but in this division I miserably imagined there to be some unknown

44

substance of irrational life, and the nature of the chief evil, which should not only be a substance, but real life also, and yet not derived from Thee, O my God, of whom are all things. And yet that first I called a Monad, as it had been a soul without sex; but the latter a Duad;—anger, in deeds of violence, and in flagitiousness, lust; not knowing whereof I spake. For I had not known or learned, that neither was evil a substance, nor our soul that chief and unchangeable good.

For as deeds of violence arise, if that emotion of the soul be corrupted, whence vehement action springs, stirring itself insolently and unrulily; and lusts, when that affection of the soul is ungoverned, create carnal pleasures; so do errors and false opinions defile the conversation, if the reasonable soul itself be corrupted; as it was then in me, who knew not that it must be enlightened by another light, that it may be partaker of truth, seeing itself is not that nature of truth. *For Thou shalt light my candle, O Lord my God, Thou shalt enlighten my darkness:* and *of Thy fulness have we all received, for Thou art the true light that lighteth every man that cometh into the world; for in Thee there is no variableness, neither shadow of change.*

But I pressed towards Thee, and was thrust from Thee, that I might taste of death: for *thou resisteth the proud.* But what prouder, than for me with a strange madness to maintain myself to be that by nature which Thou art? For whereas I was subject to change (so much being manifest to me, my very desire to become wise, being the wish, of worse to become better), yet chose I rather to imagine Thee subject to change, than myself not to be that which Thou art. Therefore I was repelled by Thee, and Thou resistedst my vain stiff-neckedness, and I imagined corporeal forms, and, myself flesh, I accused flesh; and, a *wind that passeth away, I returned not* to Thee, but I passed on and on to things which have no being, neither in Thee, nor in me, nor in the body. Neither were they created for me by Thy truth, but by my vanity devised out of things corporeal. And I was wont to ask Thy faithful little ones, my fellow-citizens (from whom, unknown to myself, I stood exiled), I was wont, prating and foolishly, to ask them, " Why then doth the soul err which God created? " But I would not be asked, " Why then doth God err? " And I maintained, that Thy unchangeable substance did err upon constraint, rather than confess that my changeable substance had gone astray voluntarily, and now, in punishment, lay in error.

I was then some six or seven and twenty years old when I wrote those volumes; revolving within me corporeal fictions, buzzing in the ears of my heart, which I turned, O sweet truth, to thy inward melody, meditating on the " fair and fit," and longing to stand and hearken to Thee, and *to rejoice greatly at the Bridegroom's voice*, but could not; for by the voices of mine own errors, I was hurried abroad, and through the weight of my own pride, I was sinking into the lowest pit. For Thou didst not *make me to hear joy and gladness*, nor did *the bones exult which were not yet humbled*.

And what did it profit me, that scarce twenty years old, a book of Aristotle, which they call the Ten Predicaments, falling into my hands (on whose very name I hung, as on something great and divine, so often as my rhetoric master of Carthage, and others, accounted learned, mouthed it with cheeks bursting with pride), I read and understood it unaided? And on my conferring with others, who said that they scarcely understood it with very able tutors, not only orally explaining it, but drawing many things in sand, they could tell me no more of it than I had learned, reading it by myself. And the book appeared to me to speak very clearly of substances, such as " man," and of their qualities, as the figure of a man, of what sort it is; and stature, how many feet high; and his relationship, whose brother he is; or where placed; or when born; or whether he stands or sits; or be shod or armed; or does, or suffers anything; and all the innumerable things which might be ranged under these nine Predicaments,[1] of which I have given some specimens, or under that chief Predicament of Substance.

[1] All the relations of things were comprised by Aristotle under nine heads; quantity, quality, relation, action, passion, where, when, situation, clothing; and these with that wherein they might be found, or " substance," ·make up the ten categories or predicaments.

What did all this further me, seeing it even hindered me? when, imagining whatever was, was comprehended under those ten Predicaments, I essayed in such wise to understand, O my God, Thy wonderful and unchangeable Unity also, *as if THOU hadst been subjected to Thine own greatness or beauty* ; so that (as in bodies) they should exist in Thee, as their subject: *whereas Thou Thyself art Thy greatness and beauty* ; but a body is not great or fair in that it is a body, seeing that, though it were less great or fair, it should notwithstanding be a body. But it was falsehood which of Thee I conceived, not truth: fictions of my misery, not the realities of Thy Blessedness. For Thou hadst commanded, and it was done in me, that the *earth should bring forth briars and thorns to me,* and that *in the sweat of my brows I should eat my bread.*

And what did it profit me, that all the books I could procure of the so-called liberal arts, I, the vile slave of vile affections, read by myself, and understood? And I delighted in them, but knew not whence came all, that therein was true or certain. For I had my back to the light, and my face to the things enlightened; whence my face, with which I discerned the things enlightened, itself was not enlightened. Whatever was written, either on rhetoric, or logic, geometry, music, and arithmetic, by myself without much difficulty or any instructor, I understood, Thou knowest, O Lord my God; because both quickness of understanding, and acuteness in discerning, is

Thy gift: yet did I not thence sacrifice to Thee. So then it served not to my use, but rather to my perdition, since I went about to get so good a *portion of my substance* into my own keeping; and I *kept not my strength for Thee,* but wandered from Thee *into a far country, to spend it upon harlotries.* For what profited me good abilities, not employed to good uses? For I felt not that those arts were attained with great difficulty, even by the studious and talented, until I attempted to explain them to such; when he most excelled in them, who followed me not altogether slowly.

But what did this further me, imagining that Thou, O Lord God, the Truth, wert a vast and bright body, and I a fragment of that body? Perverseness too great! But such was I. Nor do I blush, O my God, to *confess to Thee Thy mercies towards me,* and to call upon Thee, who blushed not then to profess to men my blasphemies, and to bark against Thee. What profited me then my nimble wit in those sciences and all those most knotty volumes, unravelled by me, without aid from human instruction; seeing I erred so foully, and with such sacrilegious shamefulness, in the doctrine of piety? Or what hindrance was a far slower wit to Thy little ones, since they departed not far from Thee, that in the nest of Thy Church they might securely be fledged, and nourish the wings of charity, by the food of a sound faith? O Lord our God, *under the shadow of Thy wings let us hope;* protect us, and carry us. Thou wilt carry us both when little, and *even to hoar hairs wilt Thou carry us*; for our firmness, when it is Thou, then is it firmness; but when our own, it is infirmity. Our good ever lives with Thee; from which when we turn away, we are turned aside. Let us now, O Lord, return, that we may not be overturned, because with Thee our good lives without any decay, which good art Thou; nor need we fear, lest there be no place whither to return, because we fell from it: for through our absence, our mansion fell not—Thy eternity.

HEALING AND REFRESHMENT

ACCEPT the sacrifice of my confessions from the ministry of my tongue, which Thou hast formed and stirred up to confess unto Thy name. *Heal Thou all my bones, and let them say, O Lord, who is like unto Thee?* For he who confesses to Thee, doth not teach Thee what takes place within him; seeing a closed heart closes not out Thy eye, nor can man's hard-heartedness thrust back Thy hand: for Thou dissolvest it at Thy will in pity or in vengeance, *and nothing can hide itself from Thy heat.* But let my soul praise Thee, that it may love Thee; and let it confess Thy own mercies to Thee, that it may praise Thee. Thy whole creation ceaseth not, nor is silent in Thy praises; neither the spirit of man with voice directed unto Thee, nor creation animate or inanimate, by the voice of those who meditate thereon: that so our souls may from their weariness arise towards Thee, leaning on those things which Thou hast created, and passing on to Thyself, who madest them wonderfully; and there is refreshment and true strength.

Let the restless, the godless, depart and flee from Thee; yet Thou seest them, and dividest the darkness. And behold, the universe with them is fair, though they are foul.[1] And how have they injured Thee? [2] or how have they disgraced Thy government, which, from the heaven to this lowest earth, is just and perfect? For whither fled they, when they fled from Thy presence? Or where dost not Thou find them? But they fled, that they might not see Thee seeing them, and, blinded, might stumble against Thee (because *Thou forsakest nothing Thou hast made*); that the unjust, I say, might stumble upon Thee, and justly be hurt; withdrawing themselves from Thy gentleness and stumbling at Thy uprightness, and falling upon their own ruggedness. Ignorant, in truth, that Thou art everywhere, whom no place encompasseth; and Thou alone art near, even to those that *remove far from Thee*. Let them then be turned, and seek Thee; because not as they have forsaken their Creator, hast Thou forsaken Thy creation. Let them be turned, and seek Thee; and behold, Thou art there in their heart, in the heart of those that confess to Thee, and cast themselves upon Thee, and weep in Thy bosom, after all their rugged ways. Then dost Thou

[1] " As a picture, wherein a black colouring occurs in its proper place, so is the universe beautiful, if any could survey it, notwithstanding the presence of sinners, although, taken by themselves, their proper deformity makes them hideous." Aug. de Civ. Dei, xi. 23.

[2] " Persons are in Scripture called the enemies of God, who, not by nature but by sins, oppose His government; able to injure, not Him, but themselves. For they are enemies through the will to resist, not through the power to hurt." *Ibid*. xii. 3.

gently wipe away their tears, and they weep the more, and joy in weeping; even for that Thou, Lord,—not man of flesh and blood, but— Thou, Lord, who madest them, re-makest and comfortest them.

* * *

But they knew not the way, Thy Word, by Whom Thou madest these things which they number, and themselves who number, and the sense whereby they perceive what they number, and the understanding, out of which they number; or that of Thy wisdom there is no number. But the Only Begotten is Himself made unto us wisdom, righteousness and sanctification, and was numbered among us, and paid tribute unto Cæsar.

They knew not the Way[1] whereby to descend to Him from themselves, and by Him ascend unto Him. They knew not the way, and deemed themselves exalted amongst the stars and shining; and behold, they *fell upon the earth, and their foolish heart was darkened*. They discourse many things truly concerning the creature; but Truth, Artificer of the creature, they seek not piously, and therefore find Him not; or if they find Him,

---

[1] " He is the home whither we go, He the way whereby we go; go we by Him to Him and we shall not go astray." Aug. Serm. 92. " Christ, as God, is the home whither we go; Christ, as man, is the way whereby we go." *Ibid.* 123. " Christ carrieth us on, as a leader, carrieth us in Him, as the way, carrieth us up to Him, as our home." Aug. in Ps. 60. sec. 4.

knowing Him to be God, they glorify Him not as God, neither are thankful, but become vain in their imaginations, and *profess themselves to be wise,* attributing to themselves what is Thine; and thereby with most perverse blindness, study to impute to Thee what is their own, forging lies of Thee who art the Truth, and *changing the glory of the uncorruptible God, into an image made like corruptible man, and to birds, and four-footed beasts, and creeping things, changing Thy truth into a lie, and worshipping and serving the creature more than the Creator.*

*   *   *

For almost all the nine years, wherein with unsettled mind I had been the disciple of the Manichæans, I had longed but too intensely for the coming of Faustus. For the rest of the sect, whom by chance I had lighted upon, when unable to solve my objections about these things, still held out to me the coming of this Faustus, by conference with whom, these and greater difficulties were to be most readily cleared. When then he came, I found him a man of pleasing discourse, who could speak fluently and in better terms, yet still but the self-same things which they were wont to say. But what availed the utmost neatness of the cup-bearer to my thirst for a more precious draught? Mine ears were already cloyed with the like, nor did they seem to me therefore better, because better said; nor therefore true, because eloquent; nor the soul therefore wise, because the face was comely, and the language graceful. But they who held him out to me, were no good judges of things; and therefore to them he appeared understanding and wise, because in words pleasing. I felt however that another sort of people were suspicious even of truth, and refused to assent to it, if delivered in a smooth and copious discourse. But Thou, O my God, hadst already taught me by wonderful and secret ways, and therefore I believe that Thou taughtest me, because it is truth, nor is there besides Thee any teacher of truth, where or whencesoever it may shine upon us. Of Thyself therefore had I now learned, that neither ought anything to seem to be spoken truly, because eloquently; nor therefore falsely, because the utterance of the lips is inharmonious; nor, again, therefore true, because rudely delivered; nor therefore false, because the language is rich; but that wisdom and folly are as wholesome and unwholesome food; and adorned or unadorned phrases as courtly or country vessels; either kind of meat may be served up in either kind of dishes.

That greediness then, wherewith I had of so long time expected that man, was delighted verily with his action and feeling when disputing, and his choice and readiness of words to clothe his ideas. I was then delighted, and, with many others and more than they, did I praise and extol him. It troubled me, however, that in the assembly of his auditors, I was not allowed to put in and communicate those questions that troubled me, in familiar converse with him. Which when I might, and with my friends began to engage his ears at such times as it was not unbecoming for him to discuss with me, I found him at first utterly ignorant of liberal sciences, save grammar, and that but in an ordinary way. But because he had read some of Tully's Orations, a very few books of Seneca, some things of the poets, and such few volumes of his own sect as were written in Latin and neatly, and was daily practised in speaking, he acquired a certain eloquence, which proved the more pleasing and seductive, because under the guidance of a good wit, and with a kind of natural gracefulness. Is it not thus, as I recall it, O Lord my God, Thou Judge of my conscience? Before Thee is my heart, and my remembrance, who didst at that time direct me by the hidden mystery of Thy providence, and didst set those shameful errors of mine before my face, that I might see and hate them.

For after it was clear, that he was ignorant of those arts in which I thought he excelled, I began to despair of his opening and solving the difficulties which perplexed me (of which indeed however ignorant, he might have held the truths of piety, had he not been a Manichee). For their books are fraught with prolix fables, of the heaven, and stars, sun, and moon, and I now no longer thought him able satisfactorily to decide what I much desired, whether, on comparison of these things with the calculations I had elsewhere read, the account given in the books of Manichæus were preferable, or at

least as good. Which when I proposed to be considered and discussed, he, so far modestly, shrunk
from the burthen. For he knew that he knew not
these things, and was not ashamed to confess it.
For he was not one of those talking persons, many
of whom I had endured, who undertook to teach
me these things, and said nothing. But this man
had a heart, though not right towards Thee, yet
neither altogether treacherous to himself. For he
was not altogether ignorant of his own ignorance,
nor would he rashly be entangled in a dispute,
whence he could neither retreat, nor extricate himself fairly. Even for this I liked him the better.
For fairer is the modesty of a candid mind, than
the knowledge of those things which I desired;
and such I found him, in all the more difficult and
subtile questions.

My zeal for the writings of Manichæus being
thus blunted, and despairing yet more of their
other teachers, seeing that in divers things which
perplexed me, he, so renowned among them, had
so turned out; I began to engage with him in the
study of that literature, on which he also was much
set (and which as rhetoric-reader I was at that time
teaching young students at Carthage), and to read
with him, either what himself desired to hear, or
such as I judged fit for his genius. But all my
efforts whereby I had purposed to advance in that
sect, upon knowledge of that man, came utterly to
an end; not that I detached myself from them
altogether, but as one finding nothing better, I had

settled to be content meanwhile with what I had in whatever way fallen upon, unless by chance something more eligible should dawn upon me. Thus that Faustus, to so many a snare of death, had now, neither willing nor witting it, begun to loosen that wherein I was taken. For Thy hands, O my God, in the secret purpose of Thy providence, did not forsake my soul; and out of my mother's heart's blood, through her tears night and day poured out, was a sacrifice offered for me unto Thee; and Thou didst deal with me by wondrous ways. Thou didst it, O my God: for *the steps of a man are ordered by the Lord, and He shall dispose his way*. Or how shall we obtain salvation, but from Thy hand, re-making what it made?

Thou didst deal with me, that I should be persuaded to go to Rome, and to teach there rather, what I was teaching at Carthage. And how I was persuaded to this, I will not neglect to confess to Thee: because herein also the deepest recesses of Thy wisdom, and Thy most present mercy to us, must be considered and confessed. I did not wish therefore to go to Rome, because higher gains and higher dignities were warranted me by my friends who persuaded me to this (though even these things had at that time an influence over my mind), but my chief and almost only reason was, that I heard that young men studied there more peacefully, and were kept quiet under a restraint of more regular discipline; so that they did not, at their pleasures, petulantly rush into the school of one whose pupils they were not, nor were even admitted without his permission. Whereas at Carthage there reigns among the scholars a most disgraceful and unruly licence. They burst in audaciously, and with gestures almost frantic, disturb all order which any one hath established for the good of his scholars. Divers outrages they commit, with a wonderful stolidity, punishable by law, did not custom uphold them; that custom evincing them to be the more miserable, in that they now do as lawful, what by Thy eternal law shall never be lawful; and they think they do it unpunished, whereas they are punished with the very blindness whereby they do it, and suffer incomparably worse than what they do. The manners then which, when a student, I would not make my own, I was fain, as a teacher, to endure in others: and so I was well pleased to go where all that knew it assured me that the like was not done. But Thou, *my refuge and my portion in the land of the living*, that I might change my earthly dwelling for the salvation of my soul, at Carthage didst goad me, that I might thereby be torn from it; and at Rome didst proffer me allurements, whereby I might be drawn thither, by men in love with a dying life, the one doing frantic, the other promising vain, things; and, to correct my steps, didst secretly use their and my own perverseness. For both they who disturbed my quiet were blinded with a disgraceful frenzy, and they who invited me elsewhere savoured of earth. And I, who here detested real misery, was there seeking unreal happiness.

But why I went hence, and went thither, Thou knewest, O God, yet showedst it neither to me, nor to my mother, who grievously bewailed my journey, and followed me as far as the sea. But I deceived her, holding me by force, that either she might keep me back, or go with me, and I feigned that I had a friend whom I could not leave, till he had a fair wind to sail. And I lied to my mother, and such a mother, and escaped: for this also hast Thou mercifully forgiven me, preserving me, thus full of execrable defilements, from the waters of the sea, for the water of Thy Grace; whereby when I was cleansed, the streams of my mother's eyes should be dried, with which for me she daily watered the ground under her face. And yet refusing to return without me, I scarcely persuaded her to stay that night in a place hard by our ship, where was an oratory in memory of the blessed Cyprian. That night I privily departed, but she was not behind in weeping and prayer. And what, O Lord, was she with so many tears asking of Thee, but that Thou wouldest not suffer me to sail? But Thou, in the depth of Thy counsels and hearing the main point of her desire, regardedst not what she then asked, that Thou mightest make me what she ever asked. The wind blew and swelled our sails, and withdrew the shore from our sight; and she on the morrow was there, frantic with sorrow, and with complaints

and groans filled Thine ears, who didst then dis-
regard them; whilst through my desires, Thou wert
hurrying me to end all desire, and the earthly part
of her affection to me was chastened by the allotted
scourge of sorrows. For she loved my being with
her, as mothers do, but much more than many;
and she knew not how great joy Thou wert about
to work for her out of my absence. She knew not;
therefore did she weep and wail, and by this agony
there appeared in her the inheritance of Eve, with
sorrow seeking what in sorrow she had brought
forth. And yet, after accusing my treachery and
hard-heartedness, she betook herself again to
intercede to Thee for me, went to her wonted
place, and I to Rome.

And lo, there was I received by the scourge of
bodily sickness, and I was going down to hell,
carrying all the sins which I had committed, both
against Thee, and myself, and others, many and
grievous, over and above that bond of original sin,
whereby *we all die in Adam*. For Thou hadst not
forgiven me any of these things in Christ, nor had
He *abolished by His cross the enmity* which by my
sins I had incurred with Thee. For how should
He, by the crucifixion of a phantasm, which I
believed Him to be? So true, then, was the death
of my soul, as that of His flesh seemed to me false;
and how true the death of His body, so false was
the life of my soul, which did not believe it. And
now the fever heightening, I was parting and
departing for ever. For had I then parted hence,

whither had I departed, but into fire and torments, such as my misdeeds deserved in the truth of Thy appointment? And this she knew not, yet in absence prayed for me. But Thou, everywhere present, heardest her where she was, and, where I was, hadst compassion upon me; that I should recover the health of my body, though frenzied as yet in my sacrilegious heart. For I did not in all that danger desire Thy baptism; and I was better as a boy, when I begged it of my mother's piety, as I have before recited and confessed. But I had grown up to my own shame, and I madly scoffed at the prescripts of Thy medicine, who wouldest not suffer me, being such, to die a double death. With which wound had my mother's heart been pierced, it could never be healed. For I cannot express the affection she bare to me, and with how much more vehement anguish she was now in labour of me in the spirit, than at her child-bearing in the flesh.

I see not then how she should have been healed, had such a death of mine stricken through the bowels of her love. And where would have been those her so strong and unceasing prayers, unintermitting to Thee alone? But wouldest Thou, God of mercies, *despise* the *contrite and humbled heart* of that chaste and sober widow, so frequent in almsdeeds, so full of duty and service to Thy saints, no day intermitting the oblation at Thine altar, twice a day, morning and evening, without any intermission, coming to Thy church, not for dle tattlings and old wives' fables; but that she might hear Thee in Thy discourses, and Thou her in her prayers. Couldest Thou despise and reject from Thy aid the tears of such an one, wherewith she begged of Thee not gold or silver, nor any mutable or passing good, but the salvation of her son's soul? Thou, by whose gift she was such? Never, Lord. Yea, Thou wert at hand, and wert hearing and doing, in that order wherein Thou hadst determined before, that it should be done. Far be it that Thou shouldest deceive her in Thy visions and answers, some whereof I have, some I have not mentioned, which she laid up in her faithful heart, and ever praying, urged upon Thee, as Thine own handwriting. For Thou, *because Thy mercy endureth for ever*, vouchsafest to those to whom Thou forgivest all their debts, to become also a debtor by Thy promises.

Thou recoveredst me then of that sickness, and healedst the son of Thy handmaid, for the time in body, that he might live, for Thee to bestow upon him a better and more abiding health. And even then, at Rome, I joined myself to those deceiving and deceived " holy ones "; not with their disciples only (of which number was he, in whose house I had fallen sick and recovered); but also with those whom they call " The *Elect*." For I still thought, " that it was not we that sin, but that I know not what other nature sinned in us "; and it delighted my pride, to be free from blame; and when I had done any evil, not to confess I had done any, *that Thou mightest heal my soul because it had sinned against Thee*: but I loved to excuse it, and to accuse I know not what other thing, which was with me, but which I was not. But in truth it was wholly I, and mine impiety had divided me against myself: and that sin was the more incurable, whereby I did not judge myself a sinner; and execrable iniquity it was, that I had rather have Thee, Thee, O God Almighty, to be overcome in me to my destruction, than myself of Thee to salvation. Not as yet then hadst Thou *set a watch before my mouth, and a door of safe keeping around my lips, that my heart might not turn aside to wicked speeches,* to *make excuses of sins, with men that work iniquity*: *and,* therefore, was I still *united with their Elect.*

MONNICA AT MILAN

O THOU, *my hope from my youth*, where wert Thou to me, and whither wert Thou gone? Hadst not Thou created me, and separated me from the beasts of the field, and fowls of the air? Thou hadst made me wiser, yet did I walk in darkness, and in slippery places, and sought Thee abroad out of myself, and found not the God of my heart; and had come into the depths of the sea, and distrusted and despaired of ever finding truth. My mother had now come to me, resolute through piety, following me over sea and land, in all perils confiding in Thee. For in perils of the sea, she comforted the very mariners (by whom passengers unacquainted with the deep, use rather to be comforted when troubled), assuring them of a safe arrival, because Thou hadst by a vision assured her thereof. She found me in grievous peril, through despair of ever finding truth. But when I had discovered to her, that I was now no longer a Manichee, though not yet a Catholic Christian, she was not overjoyed, as at something unexpected; although she was now assured concerning that part of my misery, for which she bewailed me as one dead, though to be reawakened by Thee, carrying me forth upon the *bier* of her thoughts, that Thou

mightest say to the *son of the widow, Young man,
I say unto thee, Arise; and he should revive, and
begin to speak, and Thou shouldest deliver him to his
mother.* Her heart then was shaken with no
tumultuous exultation, when she heard that what
she daily with tears desired of Thee, was already
in so great part realised; in that, though I had not
yet attained the truth, I was rescued from falsehood; but, as being assured, that Thou, who
hadst promised the whole, wouldest one day give
the rest, most calmly, and with an heart full of
confidence, she replied to me, " She believed in
Christ, that before she departed this life, she should
see me a Catholic believer." Thus much to me.
But to Thee, Fountain of mercies, poured she forth
more copious prayers and tears, that Thou wouldest
hasten Thy help, and enlighten my darkness; and
she hastened the more eagerly to the church, and
hung upon the lips of Ambrose, praying for *the
fountain of that water, which springeth up unto life
everlasting.* But that man she loved *as an angel
of God,* because she knew that by him I had been
brought for the present to that doubtful state of
faith I now was in, through which she anticipated
most confidently, that I should pass from sickness
unto health, after the access, as it were, of a sharper
fit, which physicians call " the crisis."

When then my mother had once, as she was
wont in Afric, brought to the churches built in
memory of the saints, certain cakes, and bread and
wine, and was forbidden by the door-keeper; so

soon as she knew that the bishop had forbidden
this, she so piously and obediently embraced his
wishes, that I myself wondered how readily she
censured her own practice, rather than discuss his
prohibition. For wine-bibbing did not lay siege
to her spirit, nor did love of wine provoke her to
hatred of the truth, as it doth too many (both men
and women), who revolt at a lesson of sobriety,
as men well-drunk at a draught mingled with
water. But she, when she had brought her basket
with the accustomed festival-food, to be but tasted
by herself, and then given away, never joined therewith more than one small cup of wine, diluted
according to her own abstemious habits, which
for courtesy she would taste. And if there were
many churches of the departed saints, that were
to be honoured in that manner, she still carried
round that same one cup, to be used everywhere;
and this, though not only made very watery, but
unpleasantly heated with carrying about, she would
distribute to those about her by small sips; for
she sought their devotion, not pleasure. So soon,
then, as she found this custom to be forbidden
by that famous preacher and most pious prelate,
even to those that would use it soberly, lest so an
occasion of excess might be given to the drunken;
and for that these, as it were, anniversary funeral
solemnities did much resemble the superstition of
the Gentiles. she most willingly forbare it: and
for a basket filled with fruits of the earth, she had
learned to bring to the churches of the martyrs

a breast filled with more purified petitions, and to give what she could to the poor; that so the communication of the Lord's Body might be there rightly celebrated, where, after the example of His Passion, the martyrs had been sacrificed and crowned. But yet it seems to me, O Lord my God, and thus thinks my heart of it in Thy sight, that perhaps she would not so readily have yielded to the cutting off of this custom, had it been forbidden by another, whom she loved not as Ambrose, but whom, for my salvation, she loved most entirely; and he her again, for her most religious conversation, whereby in good works, so *fervent in spirit*, she was constant at church; so that, when he saw me, he often burst forth into her praises; congratulating me, that I had such a mother; not knowing what a son she had in me, who doubted of all these things, and imagined the way to life could not be found out.

Nor did I yet groan in my prayers, that Thou wouldest help me; but my spirit was wholly intent on learning, and restless to dispute. And Ambrose himself, as the world counts happy, I esteemed a happy man, whom personages so great held in such honour; only his celibacy seemed to me a painful course. But what hope he bore within him, what struggles he had against the temptations which beset his very excellencies, or what comfort in adversities, and what sweet joys Thy Bread had for the hidden mouth of his spirit, when chewing the cud thereof, I neither could conjecture, nor had experienced. Nor did he know the tides of my feeling, or the abyss of my danger. For I could not ask of him, what I would as I would, being shut out both from his ear and speech by multitudes of busy people, whose weaknesses he served. With whom when he was not taken up (which was but a little time), he was either refreshing his body with the sustenance absolutely necessary, or his mind with reading. But when he was reading, his eye glided over the pages, and his heart searched out the sense, but his voice and tongue were at rest. Oft-times when we had come (for no man was forbidden to enter, nor was it his wont that any who came should be announced to him), we saw him thus reading to himself, and never otherwise; and having long sat silent (for who durst intrude on one so intent?), we were fain to depart.

FRIENDS

NOW I joyed that the old Scriptures of the Law and the Prophets were laid before me, not to be perused with that eye to which before they seemed absurd, when I reviled Thy holy ones for so thinking, whereas indeed they thought not so: and with joy I heard Ambrose in his sermons to the people, oftentimes most diligently recommend this text for a rule, *The letter killeth, but the Spirit giveth life*; whilst he drew aside the mystic veil, laying open spiritually what according to the letter seemed to teach something unsound; teaching herein nothing that offended me, though he taught what I knew not as yet, whether it were true. For I kept my heart from assenting to anything, fearing to fall headlong; but by hanging in suspense I was the worse killed. For I wished to be as assured of the things I saw not, as I was that seven and three are ten. For I was not so mad, as to think that even this could not be comprehended; but I desired to have other things as clear as this, whether things corporeal, which were not present to my senses, or spiritual, whereof I knew not how to conceive, except corporeally. And by believing might I have been cured, that so the eyesight of my soul being cleared, might in some way be directed to Thy truth, which abideth always, and in no part faileth. But as it happens that one who has tried a bad physician, fears to trust himself with a good one, so was it with the health of my soul, which could not be healed but by believing, and lest it should believe falsehoods, refused to be cured; resisting Thy hands, who hast prepared the medicines of faith, and hast applied them to the diseases of the whole world, and given unto them so great authority.

*　　*　　*

Since then we were too weak by abstract reasonings to find out truth: and for this very cause needed the authority of Holy Writ; I had now begun to believe, that Thou wouldest never have given such excellency of authority to that Writ in all lands, hadst Thou not willed thereby to be believed in, thereby sought. For now what things, sounding strangely in the Scripture, were wont to offend me, having heard divers of them expounded satisfactorily, I referred to the depth of the mysteries, and its authority appeared to me the more venerable, and more worthy of religious credence, in that, while it lay open to all to read, it reserved the majesty of its mysteries within its profounder meaning, stooping to all in the great plainness of its words and lowliness of its style, yet calling forth the intensest application of such as are not light of heart; that so it might receive all in its open bosom, and through narrow passages waft over towards Thee some few, yet many more than if it stood not aloft on such a height of authority, nor drew multitudes within its bosom by its holy lowliness. These things I thought on, and Thou wert with me; I sighed, and Thou heardest me; I wavered, and Thou didst guide me; I wandered through the broad way of the world, and Thou didst not forsake me.

I panted after honours, gains, marriage; and Thou deridedst me. In these desires I underwent most bitter crosses, Thou being the more gracious, the less Thou sufferedst aught to grow sweet to me, which was not Thou. Behold my heart, O Lord, who wouldest I should remember all this, and confess to Thee. Let my soul cleave unto Thee, now that Thou hast freed it from that fast-holding birdlime of death. How wretched was it! and Thou didst irritate the feeling of its wound, that forsaking all else, it might be converted unto Thee, who art above all, and without whom all things would be nothing; be converted, and be healed. How miserable was I then, and how didst Thou deal with me, to make me feel my misery on that day, when I was preparing to recite a panegyric of the Emperor,[1] wherein I *was to utter many a lie, and lying, was to be applauded by those who knew I lied, and my heart was panting* with these anxieties, and boiling with the feverishness of consuming

[1] Perhaps Valentinian the younger, whose court, according to Possidius, was at Milan, when Augustine was Professor of Rhetoric there. Augustine writes elsewhere that " he recited on the first of January a panegyric to Bauto the consul as required by his then profession of Rhetoric."

thoughts. For, passing through one of the streets of Milan, I observed a poor beggar, then, I suppose, with a full belly, joking and joyous: and I sighed, and spoke to the friends around me, of the many sorrows of our frenzies; for that by all such efforts of ours, as those wherein I *then toiled, dragging along, under the goading of desire, the burthen of my own wretchedness, and, by dragging, augmenting it, we yet looked to arrive only at that very joyousness, whither that beggar-man had arrived before us, who should never perchance attain it. For what he had obtained by means of a few begged pence, the same was I plotting by for many a toilsome turning and winding; the joy of a temporary felicity.* For he verily had not the true joy; but yet I with those my ambitious designs was seeking one much less true. And certainly he was joyous, I anxious; he void of care, I full of fears. But should any ask me, had I rather be merry or fearful? I would answer merry. Again, if he asked had I rather be such as he was, or what I then was? I should choose to be myself, though worn with cares and fears; but out of wrong judgment; for, was it the truth? For I ought not to prefer myself to him, because more learned than he, seeing I had no joy therein, but sought to please men by it; and that not to instruct, but simply to please. Wherefore also Thou didst break my bones with the staff of Thy correction.

Away with those then from my soul, who say to her, " It makes a difference, whence a man's joy is. That beggar-man joyed in drunkenness; thou

desiredst to joy in glory." What glory, Lord?
That which is not in Thee. For even as his was
no true joy, so was that no true glory: and it over-
threw my soul more. He that very night should
digest his drunkenness; but I had slept and risen
again with mine, and was to sleep again, and again
to rise with it, how many days, Thou, God, knowest. But "it doth make a difference whence a man's
joy is." I know it, and the joy of a faithful hope
lieth incomparably beyond such vanity. Yea, and
so was he then beyond me: for he verily was the
happier; not only for that he was throughly drenched
in mirth, I disembowelled with cares: but he, by
fair wishes, had gotten wine; I, by lying, was seeking
for empty, swelling praise. Much to this purpose
said I then to my friends: and I often marked in
them how it fared with me; and I found it went
ill with me, and grieved, and doubled that very ill;
and if any prosperity smiled on me, I was loth
to catch at it, for almost before I could grasp it, it
flew away.

These things we, who were living as friends
together, bemoaned together, but chiefly and most
familiarly did I speak thereof with Alypius and
Nebridius, of whom Alypius was born in the same
town with me, of persons of chief rank there, but
younger than I. For he had studied under me,
both when I first lectured in our town, and afterwards at Carthage, and he loved me much, because I seemed to him kind, and learned; and I
him, for his great towardliness to virtue, which

was eminent enough in one of no greater years. Yet the whirlpool of Carthaginian habits (amongst whom those idle spectacles are hotly followed) had drawn him into the madness of the Circus. But while he was miserably tossed therein, and I, professing rhetoric there, had a public school, as yet he used not my teaching, by reason of some unkindness risen betwixt his father and me. I had found then how dearly he doted upon the Circus, and was deeply grieved that he seemed likely to throw, or had thrown, away so great promise: yet had I no means of advising or with a sort of restraint reclaiming him, either by the kindness of a friend, or the authority of a master. For I supposed that he thought of me as did his father; but he was not such; laying aside then his father's mind in that matter, he began to greet me, come sometimes into my lecture-room, hear a little, and be gone.

I however had forgotten to deal with him, that he should not, through a blind and headlong desire of vain pastimes, undo so good a wit. But Thou, O Lord, who guidest the course of all Thou hast created, hadst not forgotten him, who was one day to be among Thy children, Priest and Dispenser of Thy Sacrament; and that his amendment might plainly be attributed to Thyself, Thou effectedst it through me, but unknowingly. For as one day I sat in my accustomed place, with my scholars before me, he entered, greeted me, sat down, and applied his mind to what I then handled. I had by chance a passage in hand, which while I was explaining, a likeness from the Circensian races occurred to me, as likely to make what I would convey pleasanter and plainer, seasoned with biting mockery of those whom that madness had enthralled; God, Thou knowest, that I then thought not of curing Alypius of that infection. But he took it wholly to himself, and thought that I had said it simply for his sake. And whence another would have taken occasion of offence with me, that right-minded youth took as a ground of being offended at himself, and loving me more fervently.

For Thou hadst said it long ago, and put it into Thy book, *Rebuke a wise man and he will love thee.* But I had not rebuked him, but Thou, who employest all, knowing or not knowing, in that order which Thyself knowest (and that order is just), didst of my heart and tongue make burning coals, by which to set on fire the hopeful mind, thus languishing, and so cure it. Let him be silent in Thy praises, who considers not Thy mercies, which confess unto Thee out of my inmost soul. For he upon that speech, burst out of that pit so deep, wherein he was wilfully plunged, and was blinded with its wretched pastimes; and he shook his mind with a strong self-command; whereupon all the filths of the Circensian pastimes flew off from him, nor came he again thither. Upon this, he prevailed with his unwilling father, that he might be my scholar. He gave way, and gave in. And Alypius beginning to be my hearer again, was involved in the same superstition with me, loving in the Manichees that show of continency which he supposed true and unfeigned. Whereas it was a senseless and seducing continency, ensnaring precious souls, unable as yet to reach the depth of virtue, yet readily beguiled with the surface of what was but a shadowy and counterfeit virtue.

He, not forsaking that secular course which his parents had charmed him to pursue, had gone before me to Rome, to study law, and there he was carried away incredibly with an incredible eagerness after the shows of gladiators. For being utterly averse to and detesting such spectacles, he was one day by chance met by divers of his acquaintance and fellow-students coming from dinner, and they with a familiar violence haled him, vehemently refusing and resisting, into the Amphitheatre, during these cruel and deadly shows, he thus protesting: " Though you hale my body to that place, and there set me, can you force me also to turn my mind or my eyes to those shows? I shall then be absent while present, and so shall overcome both you and them." They hearing this, led him on nevertheless, desirous perchance to try that very thing, whether he could do as he said. When they were come thither, and had taken their places as they could, the whole place kindled with that savage pastime. But he, closing the passages of his eyes, forbade his mind to range abroad after such evils; and would he had stopped his ears also! For in the fight, when one fell, a mighty cry of the whole people striking him strongly, overcome by curiosity, and as if prepared to despise and be superior to it whatsoever it were, even when seen, he opened his eyes, and was stricken with a deeper wound in his soul, than the other, whom he desired to behold, was in his body; and he fell more miserably than he upon whose fall that mighty noise was raised, which entered through his ears, and unlocked his eyes, to make way for the striking and beating down of a soul, bold rather than resolute, and the weaker, in that it had presumed on itself, which ought to have relied on Thee. For so soon as he saw that blood, he therewith drunk down savageness; nor turned away, but fixed his eye, drinking in frenzy, unawares, and was delighted with that guilty fight, and intoxicated with the bloody pastime. Nor was he now the man he came, but one of the throng he came unto, yea, a true associate of theirs that brought him thither. Why say more? He beheld, shouted, kindled, carried thence with him the madness which should goad him to return not only with them who first drew him thither, but also before them, yea and to draw in others. Yet thence didst Thou with a most strong and most merciful hand pluck him, and taughtest him to have confidence not in himself, but in Thee. But this was after.

But this was already being laid up in his memory to be a medicine hereafter. So was that also, that when he was yet studying under me at Carthage, and was thinking over at mid-day in the market-place what he was to say by heart (as scholars use to practise), Thou sufferedst him to be apprehended by the officers of the market-place for a thief. For no other cause, I deem, didst Thou, our God, suffer it, but that he, who was hereafter to prove so great a man, should already begin to learn, that in judging of causes, man was not readily to be condemned by man out of a rash credulity. For as he was walking up and down by himself before the judgment-seat, with his note-book and pen, lo, a young man, a lawyer, the real thief, privily bringing a hatchet, got in, unperceived by Alypius, as far as the leaden gratings, which fence in the silversmiths' shops, and began to cut away the lead. But the noise of the hatchet being heard, the silversmiths beneath began to make a stir, and sent to apprehend whomever they should find. But he hearing their voices, ran away, leaving his hatchet, fearing to be taken with it. Alypius now, who had not seen him enter, was aware of his going, and saw with what speed he made away, and being desirous to know the matter, entered the place; where finding the hatchet, he was standing, wondering and considering it, when behold, those that had been sent, find him alone with the hatchet in his hand, the noise whereof had startled and brought them thither. They seize him, hale him away, and gathering the dwellers in the market-place together, boast of having taken a notorious thief, and so he was being led away to be taken before the judge.

But thus far was Alypius to be instructed. For forthwith, O Lord, Thou succouredst his innocency, whereof Thou alone wert witness. For as he was being led either to prison or to punishment, a certain architect met them, who had the chief charge of the public buildings. Glad they were to meet him especially, by whom they were wont to be suspected of stealing the goods lost out of the market-place, as though to show him at last by whom these thefts were committed. He, however, had divers times seen Alypius at a certain senator's house, to whom he often went to pay his respects; and recognising him immediately, took him aside by the hand, and inquiring the occasion of so great a calamity, heard the whole matter, and bade all present, amid much uproar and threats, to go with him. So they came to the house of the young man who had done the deed. There, before the door, was a boy so young, as to be likely, not apprehending any harm to his master, to disclose the whole. For he had attended his master to the market-place. Whom so soon as Alypius remembered, he told the architect: and he showing the hatchet to the boy, asked him, " Whose that was? " " Ours," quoth he presently: and being further questioned, he discovered everything. Thus the crime being transferred to that house, and the multitude ashamed, which had begun to insult over Alypius. he who was to be a dispenser of Thy Word, and an examiner of many causes in Thy Church, went away better experienced and instructed.

Him then I had found at Rome, and he clave to me by a most strong tie, and went with me to Milan, both that he might not leave me, and might practise something of the law he had studied, more to please his parents than himself. There he had thrice sat as Assessor, with an uncorruptness much wondered at by others, he wondering at others rather, who could prefer gold to honesty. His character was tried besides, not only with the bait of covetousness, but with the goad of fear. At Rome he was Assessor to the Count of the Italian Treasury.[1] There was at that time a very powerful senator, to whose favours many stood indebted, whom many feared. He would needs, by his usual power, have a thing allowed him, which by the laws was unallowed. Alypius resisted it: a bribe was promised; with all his heart he scorned it: threats were held out; he trampled upon them: all wondering at so unwonted a spirit, which neither desired the friendship nor feared the enmity of one so great and so mightily renowned for innumerable means of doing good or evil. And the very judge, whose counsellor Alypius was, although also unwilling it should be, yet did not openly refuse, but put the matter off upon Alypius, alleging that he would not allow him to do it: for

[1] The Lord High Treasurer of the Western Empire was called *Comes Sacrarum largitionum*: he had six other treasurers in so many provinces under him, whereof he of Italy was one.

in truth had the judge done it, Alypius would have decided otherwise. With this one thing in the way of learning was he well-nigh seduced, that he might have books copied for him at Prætorian prices, but consulting justice, he altered his deliberation for the better; esteeming equity whereby he was hindered more gainful than the power whereby he were allowed.

These are but slight things, but *he that is faithful in little, is faithful also in much.* Nor can that anyhow be void, which proceedeth out of the mouth of Thy Truth: *If ye have not been faithful in the unrighteous Mammon, who will commit to your trust true riches? And if ye have not been faithful in that which is another man's, who shall give you that which is your own?* He, being such, did at that time cleave to me, and with me wavered in purpose, what course of life was to be taken.

Nebridius also, who having left his native country near Carthage, yea and Carthage itself, where he had much lived, leaving his excellent family-estate and house, and a mother behind, who was not to follow him, had come to Milan, for no other reason, but that with me he might live in a most ardent search after truth and wisdom. Like me he sighed, like me he wavered, an ardent searcher after true life, and a most acute examiner of the most difficult questions. Thus were there the mouths of three indigent persons, sighing out their wants one to another, and *waiting upon Thee that Thou mightest give them their meat in due season.* And in all the bitterness, which by Thy mercy followed our worldly affairs, as we looked towards the end, why we should suffer all this, darkness met us; and we turned away groaning, and saying, *How long shall these things be?* This too we often said; and so saying forsook them not, for as yet there dawned nothing certain, which, these forsaken, we might embrace.

Many of us friends conferring about, and detesting, the turbulent turmoils of human life, had debated and now almost resolved on living apart from business and the bustle of men; and this was to be thus obtained: we were to bring whatever we might severally procure, and make one household of all; so that through the truth of our friendship nothing should belong especially to any; but the whole thus derived from all, should as a whole belong to each, and all to all. We thought there might be some ten persons in this society; some of whom were very rich, especially Romanianus [1] our townsman, from childhood a

---

[1] Romanianus was a relation of Alypius, of a talent which astonished Augustine himself, " surrounded by affluence from early youth, and snatched by what are thought adverse circumstances from the absorbing whirlpools of life." Augustine frequently mentions his great wealth, as also this vexatious suit, whereby he was harassed, and which so clouded his mind, that his talents were almost unknown; as also his very great kindness to himself, when " as a poor lad, setting out to foreign study, he had received him in his house, supported, and (yet more) encouraged him; when deprived of his father, comforted, animated, aided him;

very familiar friend of mine, whom the grievous
perplexities of his affairs had brought up to court;
who was the most earnest for this project; and
therein was his voice of great weight, because his
ample estate far exceeded any of the rest. We had
settled also, that two annual officers, as it were,
should provide all things necessary, the rest being
undisturbed. But when we began to consider
whether the wives, which some of us already had,
others hoped to have, would allow this, all that
plan, which was being so well moulded, fell to
pieces in our hands, was utterly dashed and cast
aside. Thence we betook us to sighs, and groans,
and our steps to follow the *broad and beaten ways*
of the world; for many thoughts were in our
heart, *but Thy counsel standeth for ever*. Out of
which counsel Thou didst deride ours, and pre-
paredst Thine own; purposing to *give us meat in
due season, and to open Thy hand, and to fill our
souls with blessing*.

when returning from Carthage, in pursuit of a higher employ-
ment, supplied him with all necessaries "—" lastly," says
Augustine, " whatever ease I now enjoy, that I have escaped
the bonds of useless desires, that, laying aside the weight of
dead cares, I breathe, recover, return to myself, that with
all earnestness I am seeking the truth, that I am attaining
it, that I trust wholly to arrive at it, you encouraged,
impelled, effected."

THE WAY OF PERFECTION

THEN was I constrained to conceive of Thee (that incorruptible, uninjurable, and unchangeable, which I preferred before the corruptible, and injurable, and changeable) as being in space, whether infused into the world, or diffused infinitely without it. Because whatsoever I conceived, deprived of this space, seemed to me nothing, yea altogether nothing, not even a void, as if a body were taken out of its place, and the place should remain empty of any body at all, of earth and water, air and heaven, yet would it remain a void place, as it were a spacious nothing.

I then being thus gross-hearted, nor clear even to myself, whatsoever was not extended over certain spaces, nor diffused, nor condensed, nor swelled out, or did not or could not receive some of these dimensions, I thought to be altogether nothing. For over such forms as my eyes are wont to range, did my heart then range: nor yet did I see that this same notion of the mind, whereby I formed those very images, was not of this sort, and yet it could not have formed them, had not itself been some great thing. So also did I endeavour to conceive of Thee, Life of my life, as vast, through infinite spaces, on every side penetrating the whole mass of the universe, and beyond it, every way, through unmeasurable boundless spaces; so that the earth should have Thee, the heaven have Thee, all things have Thee, and they be bounded in Thee, and Thou bounded nowhere. For that as the body of this air which is above the earth, hindereth not the light of the sun from passing through it, penetrating it, not by bursting or by cutting, but by filling it wholly: so I thought the body not of heaven, air, and sea only, but of the earth too, pervious to Thee, so that in all its parts, the greatest as the smallest, it should admit Thy presence, by a secret inspiration, within and without, directing all things which Thou hast created. So I guessed, only as unable to conceive aught else, for it was false. For thus should a greater part of the earth contain a greater portion of Thee, and a less, a lesser: and all things should in such sort be full of Thee, that the body of an elephant should contain more of Thee than that of a sparrow, by how much larger it is, and takes up more room; and thus shouldest Thou make the several portions of Thyself present unto the several portions of the world, in fragments, large to the large, petty to the petty. But such art not Thou. But not as yet hadst Thou enlightened my darkness.

*　　*　　*

Thou being my Guide, and become my Helper, I entered and beheld with the eye of my soul (such as it was), above the same eye of my soul, above my mind, the Light Unchangeable. Not this ordinary light, which all flesh may look upon, nor as it were a greater of the same kind, as though the brightness of this should be manifold brighter, and with its greatness take up all space. Not such was this light, but other, yea, far other from all these. Nor was it above my soul, as oil is above water, nor yet as heaven above earth: but above to my soul, because It made me; and I below It, because I was made by It. He that knows the Truth, knows what that Light is; and he that knows It, knows eternity. Love knoweth it. O Truth who art Eternity! and Love who art Truth! and Eternity who art Love! Thou art my God, to Thee do I sigh night and day. Thee when I first knew, Thou liftedst me up, that I might see there was what I might see, and that I was not yet such as to see. And Thou didst beat back the weakness of my sight, streaming forth Thy beams of light upon me most strongly, and I trembled with love and awe: and I perceived myself to be far off from Thee, in the region of unlikeness, as if I heard this Thy voice from on high: " I am the food of grown men; grow, and thou shalt feed upon Me; nor shalt thou convert Me, like the food of thy flesh, into thee, but thou shalt be converted into Me." And I learned, that *Thou for iniquity chastenest man, and Thou madest my soul to consume away like a spider*. And I said, " Is Truth therefore nothing because it is not diffused through space finite or infinite?" And Thou criedst to

me from afar: " Yea, verily, *I AM that I AM.*"
And I heard, as the heart heareth, nor had I
room to doubt, and I should sooner doubt that I
live, than that Truth is not, *which is clearly seen,
being understood by those things which are made.*

And I beheld the other things below Thee, and
I perceived that they neither altogether are, nor
altogether are not, for they are, since they are from
Thee, but are not, because they are not what Thou
art. *For that truly is, which remains unchangeably.
It is then good for me to hold fast unto God; for
if I remain not in Him, I cannot in myself; but
He remaining in Himself, reneweth all things. And
Thou art the Lord my God, since Thou standest
not in need of my goodness.*

* * *

Now I wondered that I loved Thee, and no
phantasm for Thee. And yet did I not press on to
enjoy my God; but was borne up to Thee by Thy
beauty, and soon borne down from Thee by mine
own weight, sinking with sorrow into these inferior
things. This weight was carnal custom. Yet
dwelt there with me a remembrance of Thee; nor
did I any way doubt, that there was One to whom
I might cleave, but that I was not yet such as to
cleave to Thee: for that *the body which is corrupted,
presseth down the soul, and the earthly tabernacle
weigheth down the mind that museth upon many
things.* And most certain I was, *that Thy invisible
works from the creation of the world are clearly seen,*

*being understood by the things that are made, even
Thy eternal power and Godhead.* For examining,
whence it was that I admired the beauty of bodies
celestial or terrestrial; and what aided me in
judging soundly on things mutable, and pronouncing, "This ought to be thus, this not";
examining, I say, whence it was that I so judged,
seeing I did so judge, I had found the unchangeable and true Eternity of Truth, above my changeable mind. And thus by degrees I passed from
bodies to the soul, which through the bodily senses
perceives; and thence to its inward faculty, to
which the bodily senses represent things external,
whitherto reach the faculties of beasts; and
thence again to the reasoning faculty, to which
what is received from the senses of the body, is
referred to be judged. Which finding itself also to
be in me a thing variable, raised itself up to its own
understanding, and drew away my thoughts from
the power of habit, withdrawing itself from those
troops of contradictory phantasms; that so it
might find what that light was, whereby it was
bedewed, when, without all doubting, it cried out,
"That the unchangeable was to be preferred to
the changeable"; whence also it knew That Unchangeable, which, unless it had in some way
known, it had had no sure ground to prefer it to
the changeable. And thus with the flash of one
trembling glance it arrived at THAT WHICH IS.
And then I saw Thy *invisible things understood
by the things which are made.* But I could not fix

my gaze thereon; and my infirmity being struck back, I was thrown again on my wonted habits, carrying along with me only a loving memory thereof, and a longing for what I had, as it were, perceived the odour of, but was not yet able to feed on.

Then I sought a way of obtaining strength, sufficient to enjoy Thee; and found it not, until I embraced *that Mediator betwixt God and men, the Man Christ Jesus, who is over all, God blessed for evermore,* calling unto me, and saying, *I am the way, the truth, and the life,* and mingling that food which I was unable to receive, with our flesh. *For the Word was made flesh,* that Thy wisdom, whereby Thou createdst all things, might provide milk for our infant state. For I did not hold to my Lord Jesus Christ, I, humbled, to the Humble; nor knew I yet whereto His infirmity would guide us. For Thy Word, the Eternal Truth, far above the higher parts of Thy Creation, raises up the subdued unto Itself: but in this lower world built for Itself a lowly habitation of our clay, whereby to abase from themselves such as would be subdued, and bring them over to Himself; allaying their swelling, and fomenting their love; to the end they might go on no further in self-confidence, but rather consent to become weak, seeing before their feet the Divinity weak by taking our *coats of skin*; [1]

[1] " The 'skin' denotes mortality; wherefore our first parents, the authors of the sin of the human race, having become mortal, were dismissed from paradise; but to denote

and wearied, might cast themselves down upon It, and It rising, might lift them up.

But I thought otherwise; conceiving only of my Lord Christ as of a man of excellent wisdom, whom no one could be equalled unto; especially, for that being wonderfully born of a Virgin, He seemed, in conformity therewith, through the Divine care for us, to have attained that great eminence of authority, for an ensample of despising things temporal for the obtaining of immortality. But what mystery there lay in " *The Word was made flesh*," I could not even imagine. Only I had learnt out of what is delivered to us in writing of Him—that He did eat, and drink, sleep, walk, rejoiced in spirit, was sorrowful, discoursed—that flesh did not cleave by itself unto Thy Word, but with the human soul and mind. All know this, who know the unchangeableness of Thy Word, which I now knew, as far as I could, nor did I at all doubt thereof. For, now to move the limbs of the body by will, now not, now to be moved by some affection, now not, now to deliver wise sayings through human signs, now to keep silence, belong to soul and mind subject to variation. And should these things be falsely written of Him, all the rest also would risk the charge, nor would there remain in those books any saving faith for mankind. Since then they were written truly, I acknowledged

their mortality, they were clothed with ' coats of skins ' ; skins are only taken from dead animals ; therefore by the name of skins, that mortality was figured."

a perfect man to be in Christ; not the body of a man only, nor, with the body, a sensitive soul without a rational, but very man; whom, not only as being a form of Truth, but for a certain great excellency of human nature and a more perfect participation of wisdom, I judged to be preferred before all others.

SIMPLICIANUS

TO Simplicianus then I went, the father of Ambrose (a Bishop now) in receiving Thy grace, and by Ambrose truly loved as a father. To him I related the mazes of my wanderings. But when I mentioned that I had read certain books of the Platonists, which Victorinus, sometime Rhetoric Professor of Rome (who had died a Christian, as I had heard), had translated into Latin, he testified his joy that I had not fallen upon the writings of other philosophers, full of *fallacies and deceits, after the rudiments of this world*, whereas the Platonists many ways led to the belief in God, and His Word. Then to exhort me to the humility of Christ, *hidden from the wise, and revealed to little ones*, he spoke of Victorinus himself, whom while at Rome he had most intimately known: and of him he related what I will not conceal. For it contains great *praise of Thy grace*, to be confessed unto Thee, how that aged man, most learned and skilled in the liberal sciences, and who had read, and weighed so many works of the philosophers; the instructor of so many noble senators, who also, as a monument of his excellent discharge of his office, had (which men of this world esteem a high

honour) both deserved and obtained a statue in the
Roman Forum; he, to that age a worshipper of
idols, and a partaker of the sacrilegious rites, to
which almost all the nobility of Rome were given
up, and had inspired the people with the love of

> Anubis, barking Deity, and all
> The monster Gods of every kind, who fought
> 'Gainst Neptune, Venus, and Minerva;

whom Rome once conquered, now adored, all
which the aged Victorinus had with thundering
eloquence so many years defended;— he now
blushed not to be the child of Thy Christ, and the
new-born babe of Thy fountain; submitting his
neck to the yoke of humility, and subduing his
forehead to the reproach of the Cross.

O Lord, Lord, *Which hast bowed the heavens
and come down, touched the mountains and they did
smoke,* by what means didst Thou convey Thyself
into that breast? He used to read (as Simplicianus
said) the holy Scripture, most studiously sought
and searched into all the Christian writings, and
said to Simplicianus (not openly, but privately
and as a friend), " Understand that I am already
a Christian." Whereto he answered, " I will not
believe it, nor will I rank you among Christians,
unless I see you in the Church of Christ." The
other, in banter, replied, " Do walls then make
Christians?" And this he often said, that he was
already a Christian; and Simplicianus as often
made the same answer, and the conceit of the
" walls " was by the other as often renewed. For

he feared to offend his friends, proud demon-worshippers, from the height of whose Babylonian dignity, as from *cedars of Libanus*, which *the Lord* had not yet *broken down*, he supposed the weight of enmity would fall upon him. But after that by reading and earnest thought he had gathered firmness, and feared to be *denied by Christ before the holy angels, should he now be afraid to confess him before men*, and appeared to himself guilty of a heavy offence, in being ashamed of the Sacraments of the humility of Thy Word, and not being ashamed of the sacrilegious rites of those proud demons, whose pride he had imitated and their rites adopted, he became bold-faced against vanity, and shame-faced towards the truth, and suddenly and unexpectedly said to Simplicianus (as himself told me), " Go we to the Church; I wish to be made a Christian." But he, not containing himself for joy, went with him. And having been admitted to the first Sacrament and become a Catechumen, not long after he further gave in his name, that he might be regenerated by baptism, Rome wondering, the Church rejoicing. The proud *saw, and were wroth; they gnashed with their teeth, and melted away*. But the *Lord* God *was the hope* of Thy servant, and *he regarded not vanities and lying* madness.

To conclude, when the hour was come for making profession of his faith (which at Rome they, who are about to approach to Thy grace, deliver, from an elevated place, in sight of all the faithful, in a set form of words committed to memory), the presbyters, he said, offered Victorinus (as was done to such as seemed likely through bashfulness to be alarmed) to make his profession more privately: but he chose rather to profess his salvation in the presence of the holy multitude. " For it was not salvation that he taught in rhetoric, and yet that he had publicly professed. How much less then ought he, when pronouncing Thy word, to dread Thy meek flock, who, when delivering his own words, had not feared a mad multitude! " When, then, he went up to make his profession, all, as they knew him, whispered his name one to another with the voice of congratulation. And who there knew him not? and there ran a low murmur through all the mouths of the rejoicing multitude, Victorinus! Victorinus! Sudden was the burst of rapture, that they saw him; suddenly were they hushed that they might hear him. He pronounced the true faith with an excellent boldness, and all wished to draw him into their very heart: yea by their love and joy they drew him thither; such were the hands wherewith they drew him.

Good God! what takes place in man, that he should more rejoice at the salvation of a soul despaired of, and freed from greater peril, than if there had always been hope of him, or the danger had been less? For so Thou also, merciful Father, *dost more rejoice over one penitent, than over ninety-nine just persons, that need no repentance.* And with much joyfulness do we hear, so often as we hear with what joy *the sheep which had strayed is brought back upon the shepherd's shoulder*, and *the groat is restored to Thy treasury, the neighbours rejoicing with the woman who found it*; and the joy of the solemn service of Thy house forceth to tears, when in Thy house it is read of Thy *younger son, that he was dead, and lived again; had been lost, and is found*. For Thou *rejoicest* in us, and in Thy holy angels, holy through holy charity. For Thou art ever the same; for all things which abide not the same nor for ever, Thou for ever knowest in the same way.

What then takes place in the soul, when it is more delighted at finding or recovering the things it loves, than if it had ever had them? yea, and other things witness hereunto; and all things are full of witnesses, crying out, " So is it." The conquering commander triumpheth; yet had he not conquered, unless he had fought; and the more peril there was in the battle, so much the more joy is there in the triumph. The storm tosses the sailors, threatens shipwreck; all wax pale at approaching death; sky and sea are calmed, and they are exceeding joyed, as having been exceeding afraid. A friend is sick, and his pulse threatens danger; all who long for his recovery are sick in mind with him. He is restored, though as yet he walks not with his former strength; yet there is such joy, as was not, when before he walked sound and strong. Yea, the very pleasures of human life men acquire by difficulties, not those only which fall upon us unlooked for, and against our wills, but even by self-chosen and pleasure-seeking trouble. Eating and drinking have no pleasure, unless there precede the pinching of hunger and thirst. Men, given to drink, eat certain salt meats, to procure a troublesome heat, which the drink allaying, causes pleasure. It is also ordered, that the affianced bride should not at once be given, lest as a husband he should hold cheap whom, as betrothed, he sighed not after.

This law holds in foul and accursed joy; this in permitted and lawful joy; this in the very purest perfection of friendship; this in him *who was dead, and lived again; had been lost, and was found.* Everywhere the greater joy is ushered in by the greater pain. What means this, O Lord my God, whereas Thou art everlastingly joy to Thyself, and some things around Thee evermore rejoice in Thee? What means this, that this portion of things thus ebbs and flows alternately displeased and reconciled? Is this their allotted measure? Is this all Thou hast assigned to them, whereas from the highest heavens to the lowest earth, from the beginning of the world to the end of ages, from the angel to the worm, from the first motion to the last, Thou settest each in its place, and realisest each in their season, everything good after its kind? Woe is me! how high art Thou in the highest, and how deep in the deepest! and Thou never departest, and we scarcely return to Thee.

Up, Lord, and do; stir us up, and recall us; kindle and draw us; inflame, grow sweet unto us;

let us now love, *let us run*. Do not many, out of a deeper hell of blindness than Victorinus, return to Thee, approach, and are enlightened, receiving that *Light*, which *they who receive, receive power from Thee to become Thy sons?*

THE DEATH OF MONNICA

MY confessions and thanksgivings receive, O my God for innumerable things whereof I am silent. But I will not omit whatsoever my soul would bring forth concerning that Thy handmaid, who brought me forth, both in the flesh, that I might be born to this temporal light, and in heart, that I might be born to Light eternal.[1] Not her gifts, but Thine in her, would I speak of; for neither did she make nor educate herself. Thou createdst her; nor did her father and mother know what a one should come from them. And the sceptre of Thy Christ, the discipline of Thine only Son, in a Christian house, a good member of Thy Church, educated her in Thy fear. Yet for her good discipline, was she wont to commend not so much her mother's diligence, as that of a certain decrepit

---

[1] Augustine thus addressed his mother (De Vita Beata), "You, through whose prayers I undoubtingly believe and affirm, that God gave me that mind that I should prefer nothing to the discovery of truth, wish, think of, love, nought besides. Nor do I fail to believe, that this so great good, which, through thee, I have come to desire, through thy prayers I shall attain"; and says of her, "chiefly my mother, to whom, I believe, I owe all which in me is life," and long after (De Dono Persev., sec. 35), "that to the faithful and daily tears of my mother, I was granted, that I should not perish."

maid-servant, who had carried her father when a child, as little ones use to be carried at the backs of elder girls. For which reason, and for her great age, and excellent conversation, was she, in that Christian family, well respected by its heads. Whence also the charge of her master's daughters was entrusted to her, to which she gave diligent heed, restraining them earnestly, when necessary, with a holy severity, and teaching them with a grave discretion. For, except at those hours wherein they were most temperately fed at their parents' table, she would not suffer them, though parched with thirst, to drink even water; preventing an evil custom, and adding this wholesome advice: "Ye drink water now, because you have not wine in your power; but when you come to be married, and be made mistresses of cellars and cupboards, you will scorn water, but the custom of drinking will abide." By this method of instruction, and the authority she had, she refrained the greediness of childhood, and moulded their very thirst to such an excellent moderation, that what they should not, that they would not.

And yet (as Thy handmaid told me her son) there had crept upon her a love of wine. For when (as the manner was) she, as though a sober maiden, was bidden by her parents to draw wine out of the hogshead, holding the vessel under the opening, before she poured the wine into the flagon, she sipped a little with the tip of her lips; for more her instinctive feelings refused. For this she did, not out of any desire of drink, but out of the exuberance of youth, whereby it boils over in mirthful freaks, which in youthful spirits are wont to be kept under by the gravity of their elders. And thus by adding to that little, daily littles (*for whoso despiseth little things, shall fall by little and little*), she had fallen into such a habit, as greedily to drink off her little cup brimful almost of wine. Where was then that discreet old woman, and that her earnest countermanding? Would aught avail against a secret disease, if Thy healing hand, O Lord, watched not over us? Father, mother, and governors absent, Thou present, who createdst, who callest, who also by those set over us, workest something towards the salvation of our souls, what didst Thou then, O my God? how didst Thou cure her? how heal her? didst Thou not out of another soul bring forth a hard and a sharp taunt, like a lancet out of Thy secret store, and with one touch remove all that foul stuff? For a maid-servant with whom she used to go to the cellar, falling to words (as it happens) with her little mistress, when alone with her, taunted her with this fault, with most bitter insult, calling her wine-bibber. With which taunt she, stung to the quick, saw the foulness of her fault, and instantly condemned and forsook it. As flattering friends pervert, so reproachful enemies mostly correct. Yet not what by them Thou doest, but what themselves purposed, dost Thou repay them. For she in her anger sought to vex her young mistress, not to amend her;

and did it in private, either for that the time and
place of the quarrel so found them; or lest herself
also should have anger, for discovering it thus
late. But Thou, Lord, Governor of all in heaven
and earth, who turnest to Thy purposes the deepest
currents, and the ruled turbulence of the tide of
times, didst by the very unhealthiness of one soul
heal another; lest any, when he observes this,
should ascribe it to his own power, even when
another, whom he wished to be reformed, is
reformed through words of his.

Brought up thus modestly and soberly, and made
subject rather by Thee to her parents, than by her
parents to Thee, so soon as she was of marriageable
age, being bestowed upon a husband, she served
him as her lord; and did her diligence to win
him unto Thee, preaching Thee unto him by her
conversation; by which Thou ornamentedst her,
making her reverently amiable, and admirable unto
her husband. And she so endured the wronging
of her bed, as never to have any quarrel with her
husband thereon. For she looked for Thy mercy
upon him, that believing in Thee, he might be
made chaste. But besides this, he was fervid, as
in his affections, so in anger: but she had learnt
not to resist an angry husband, not in deed only,
but not even in word. Only when he was smoothed
and tranquil, and in a temper to receive it, she would
give an account of her actions, if haply he had
overhastily taken offence. In a word, while many
matrons, who had milder husbands, yet bore even

in their faces marks of shame, would in familiar talk blame their husbands' lives, she would blame their tongues, giving them, as in jest, earnest advice: "That from the time they heard the marriage writings read to them, they should account them as indentures, whereby they were made servants; and so, remembering their condition, ought not to set themselves up against their lords." And when they, knowing what a choleric husband she endured, marvelled that it had never been heard, nor by any token perceived, that Patricius had beaten his wife, or that there had been any domestic difference between them, even for one day, and confidentially asked the reason, she taught them her practice above mentioned. Those wives who observed it found the good, and returned thanks; those who observed it not, found no relief, and suffered.

Her mother-in-law also, at first by whisperings of evil servants incensed against her, she so overcame by observance and persevering endurance and meekness, that she of her own accord discovered to her son the meddling tongues, whereby the domestic peace betwixt her and her daughter-in-law had been disturbed, asking him to correct them. Then, when in compliance with his mother, and for the well-ordering of the family, and the harmony of its members, he had with stripes corrected those discovered, at her will who had discovered them, she promised the like reward to any who, to please her, should speak ill of her daughter-in-law to her: and, none now venturing, they lived together with a remarkable sweetness of mutual kindness.

This great gift also Thou bestowedst, O my God, my mercy, upon that good handmaid of Thine, in whose womb Thou createdst me, that between any disagreeing and discordant parties where she was able, she showed herself such a peacemaker, that hearing on both sides most bitter things, such as swelling and indigested choler uses to break out into, when the crudities of enmities are breathed out in sour discourses to a present friend against an absent enemy, she never would disclose aught of the one unto the other, but what might tend to their reconcilement. A small good this might appear to me, did I not to my grief know numberless persons, who through some horrible and wide-spreading contagion of sin, not only disclose to persons mutually angered things said in anger, but add withal things never spoken, whereas to humane humanity, it ought to seem a light thing, not to foment or increase ill will by ill words, unless one study withal by good words to quench it. Such was she, Thyself, her most inward Instructor, teaching her in the school of the heart.

Finally, her own husband, towards the very end of his earthly life, did she gain unto Thee; nor had she to complain of that in him as a believer, which before he was a believer she had borne from him. She was also the servant of Thy servants; whosoever of them knew her, did in her much praise and honour and love Thee; for that through the witness of the fruits of a holy conversation they perceived Thy presence in her heart. For she had been *the wife of one man*, had *requited her parents, had governed her house* piously, *was well reported of for good works, had brought up children,* so often *travailing in birth of them*, as she saw them swerving from Thee. Lastly, of all of us Thy servants, O Lord (whom on occasion of Thy own gift Thou sufferest to speak), us, who before her sleeping in Thee lived united together, having received the grace of Thy baptism, did she so take care of, as though she had been mother of us all; so served us, as though she had been child to us all.

The day now approaching whereon she was to depart this life (which day Thou well knewest, we knew not), it came to pass, Thyself, as I believe, by Thy secret ways so ordering it, that she and I stood alone, leaning in a certain window, which looked into the garden of the house where we now lay, at Ostia; where removed from the din of men, we were recruiting from the fatigues of a long journey, for the voyage. We were discoursing then together, alone, very sweetly; and *forgetting those things which are behind, and reaching forth unto those things which are before*, we were inquiring between ourselves in the presence of the Truth, which Thou art, of what sort the eternal life of the saints was to be, *which eye hath not seen, nor ear heard, nor hath it entered into the heart of man.*

But yet we gasped with the mouth of our heart, after those heavenly streams of Thy fountain, *the fountain of life*, which is *with Thee*; that being bedewed thence according to our capacity, we might in some sort meditate upon so high a mystery.

And when our discourse was brought to that point, that the very highest delight of the earthly senses, in the very purest material light, was, in respect of the sweetness of that life, not only not worthy of comparison, but not even of mention; we raising up ourselves with a more glowing affection towards the " Self-same," did by degrees pass through all things bodily, even the very heaven, whence sun and moon and stars shine upon the earth; yea, we were soaring higher yet, by inward musing, and discourse, and admiring of Thy works; and we came to our own minds, and went beyond them, that we might arrive at that region of never-failing plenty, where *Thou feedest Israel* for ever with the food of truth, and where life is the *Wisdom by whom all* these *things are made*, and what have been, and what shall be, and she is not made, but is, as she hath been, and so shall she be ever; yea rather, to " have been," and " hereafter to be," are not in her, but only " to be," seeing she is eternal. For to " have been," and to " be hereafter," are not eternal. And while we were discoursing and panting after her, we slightly touched on her with the whole effort of our heart; and we sighed, and there we left bound *the first fruits of the Spirit*; and returned to vocal expressions of our mouth, where the word spoken has beginning and end. And what is like unto Thy Word, our Lord, who *endureth in Himself* without becoming old, and *maketh all things new*?

We were saying then: If to any the tumult of the flesh were hushed, hushed the images of earth, and waters, and air, hushed also the poles of heaven, yea the very soul be hushed to herself, and by not thinking on self surmount self, hushed all dreams and imaginary revelations, every tongue and every sign, and whatsoever exists only in transition, since if any could hear, all these say, *We made not ourselves, but He made us that abideth for ever*—If then having uttered this, they too should be hushed, having roused only our ears to Him who made them, and He alone speak, not by them, but by Himself, that we may hear His Word, not through any tongue of flesh, nor angel's voice, nor sound of thunder, nor in the dark riddle of a similitude, but, might hear Whom in these things we love, might hear His Very Self without these (as we two now strained ourselves, and in swift thought touched on that Eternal Wisdom, which abideth over all);—could this be continued on, and other visions of kind far unlike be withdrawn, and this one ravish, and absorb, and wrap up its beholder amid these inward joys, so that life might be for ever like that one moment of understanding which now we sighed after; were not this, *Enter into thy Master's joy*? And when shall that be?

When *we shall all rise again*, though we *shall not all be changed?*

Such things was I speaking, and even if not in this very manner, and these same words, yet, Lord, Thou knowest, that in that day when we were speaking of these things, and this world with all its delights became, as we spake, contemptible to us, my mother said, " Son, for mine own part I have no further delight in anything in this life. What I do here any longer, and to what end I am here, I know not, now that my hopes in this world are accomplished. One thing there was, for which I desired to linger for a while in this life, that I might see thee a Catholic Christian before I died. My God hath done this for me more abundantly, that I should now see thee withal, despising earthly happiness, become His servant: what do I here? "

What answer I made her unto these things, I remember not. For scarce five days after, or not much more, she fell sick of a fever; and in that sickness one day she fell into a swoon, and was for a while withdrawn from these visible things. We hastened round her; but she was soon brought back to her senses; and looking on me and my brother [1] standing by her, said to us inquiringly, " Where was I? " And then looking fixedly on us, with grief amazed: " Here," saith she, " shall you bury your mother." I held my peace and refrained weeping; but my brother spake something, wishing for her, as the happier lot, that she might

[1] His name was Navigius.

die, not in a strange place, but in her own land. Whereat, she with anxious look, checking him with her eyes, for that he still *savoured such things*, and then looking upon me : " Behold," saith she, " what he saith ": and soon after to us both, " Lay," she saith, " this body anywhere; let not the care for that any way disquiet you: this only I request, that you would remember me at the Lord's altar, wherever you be." And having delivered this sentiment in what words she could, she held her peace, being exercised by her growing sickness.

But I, considering Thy gifts, Thou unseen God, which Thou instillest into the hearts of Thy faithful ones, whence wondrous fruits do spring, did rejoice and give thanks to Thee, recalling what I before knew, how careful and anxious she had ever been as to her place of burial, which she had provided and prepared for herself by the body of her husband. For because they had lived in great harmony together, she also wished (so little can the human mind embrace things divine) to have this addition to that happiness, and to have it remembered among men, that after her pilgrimage beyond the seas, what was earthly of this united pair had been permitted to be united beneath the same earth. But when this emptiness had through the fulness of Thy goodness begun to cease in her heart, I knew not, and rejoiced admiring what she had disclosed to me; though indeed in that our discourse also in the window, when she said, " What do I here any longer? " there appeared no desire of dying in her own country. I heard afterwards also, that when we were at Ostia, she with a mother's confidence, when I was absent, one day discoursed with certain of my friends about the contempt of this life, and the blessing of death: and when they were amazed at such courage which Thou hadst given to a woman, and asked "Whether she were not afraid to leave her body so far from her own city?" she replied, "Nothing is far to God; nor was it to be feared lest at the end of the world, He should not recognise whence He were to raise me up." On the ninth day then of her sickness, and the fifty-sixth year of her age, and the three-and-thirtieth of mine, was that religious and holy soul freed from the body.

I closed her eyes; and there flowed withal a mighty sorrow into my heart, which was overflowing into tears; mine eyes at the same time, by the violent command of my mind, drank up their fountain wholly dry; and woe was me in such a strife! But when she breathed her last, the boy Adeodatus burst out into a loud lament; then, checked by us all, held his peace. In like manner also a childish feeling in me, which was, through my heart's youthful voice, finding its vent in weeping, was checked and silenced. For we thought it not fitting to solemnise that funeral with tearful lament, and groanings: for thereby do they for the most part express grief for the departed, as though unhappy, or altogether dead; whereas she was neither unhappy in her death, nor altogether dead.

Of this we were assured on good grounds, the testimony of her good conversation and her *faith unfeigned*.

What then was it which did grievously pain me within, but a fresh wound wrought through the sudden wrench of that most sweet and dear custom of living together? I joyed indeed in her testimony, when, in that her last sickness, mingling her endearments with my acts of duty, she called me " dutiful," and mentioned, with great affection of love, that she never had heard any harsh or reproachful sound uttered by my mouth against her. But yet, O my God, who madest us, what comparison is there betwixt that honour that I paid to her, and her slavery for me? Being then forsaken of so great comfort in her, my soul was wounded, and that life rent asunder as it were, which, of hers and mine together, had been made but one.

The boy then being stilled from weeping, Euodius took up the Psalter, and began to sing, our whole house answering him, the Psalm, *I will sing of mercy and judgment to Thee, O Lord*. But hearing what we were doing, many brethren and religious women came together; and whilst they (whose office it was) made ready for the burial, as the manner is, I (in a part of the house where I might properly), together with those who thought not fit to leave me, discoursed upon something fitting the time; and by this balm of truth, assuaged that torment, known to Thee, they unknowing and listening intently, and conceiving me to be without all sense of sorrow. But in Thy ears, where none of them heard, I blamed the weakness of my feelings, and refrained my flood of grief, which gave way a little unto me; but again came, as with a tide, yet not so as to burst out into tears, nor to a change of countenance; still I knew what I was keeping down in my heart. And being very much displeased, that these human things had such power over me, which in the due order and appointment of our natural condition must needs come to pass, with a new grief I grieved for my grief, and was thus worn by a double sorrow.

And behold, the corpse was carried to the burial; we went and returned without tears. For neither in those prayers which we poured forth unto Thee, when the sacrifice of our ransom was offered for her, when now the corpse was by the grave's side, as the manner there is, previous to its being laid therein, did I weep even during those prayers; yet was I the whole day in secret heavily sad, and with troubled mind prayed Thee, as I could, to heal my sorrow, yet Thou didst not; impressing, I believe, upon my memory by this one instance, how strong is the bond of all habit, even upon a soul which now feeds upon no deceiving Word. It seemed also good to me to go and bathe, having heard that the bath had its name (balneum) from the Greek βαλανεῖον, for that it drives sadness from the mind. And this also I confess unto Thy mercy, *Father of the fatherless*, that I bathed, and was the same as before I bathed. For the bitterness of sorrow could not exude out of my heart. Then I slept, and woke up again, and found my grief not a little softened; and as I was alone in my bed, I remembered those true verses of Thy Ambrose. For Thou art the

Maker of all, the Lord and Ruler of the height,
Who, robing day in light, hast poured soft slumbers o'er the night,
That to our limbs the power of toil may be renewed,
And hearts be rais'd that sink and cower, and sorrows be subdued.

And then by little and little I recovered my former thoughts of Thy handmaid, her holy conversation towards Thee, her holy tenderness and observance towards us, whereof I was suddenly deprived; and I was minded to weep in Thy sight, for her and for myself, in her behalf and in my own. And I gave way to the tears which I before restrained, to overflow as much as they desired; reposing my heart upon them; and it found rest in them, for it was in Thy eyes, not in those of man, who would have scornfully interpreted my weeping. And now, Lord, in writing I confess it unto Thee. Read it, who will, and interpret it, how he will: and if he finds sin therein, that I wept my mother for a small portion of an hour (the mother who for the time was dead to mine eyes, who had for many years wept for me, that I might live in Thine eyes), let him not deride me; but rather, if he be one of large charity, let him weep himself for my sins unto Thee, the Father of all the brethren of Thy Christ.

But now, with a heart cured of that wound, wherein it might seem blameworthy for an earthly feeling, I pour out unto Thee, our God, in behalf of that Thy handmaid, a far different kind of tears, flowing from a spirit shaken by the thoughts of the dangers of every soul *that dieth in Adam.* And although she having been quickened in Christ, even before her release from the flesh, had lived to the praise of Thy name for her faith and conversation; yet dare I not say that from what time Thou regeneratedst her by baptism, no word issued from her mouth against Thy Commandment. Thy Son, the Truth, hath said, *Whosoever shall say unto his brother, Thou fool, shall be in danger of hell fire.* And woe be even unto the commendable life of men, if, laying aside mercy, Thou shouldest examine it. But because Thou art not extreme in inquiring after sins, we confidently hope to find some place with Thee. But whosoever reckons up his real merits to Thee, what reckons he up to Thee, but Thine own gifts? O that men would know themselves to be men; *and that he that glorieth, would glory in the Lord.*

I therefore, O my Praise and my Life, God of my heart, laying aside for a while her good deeds, for which I give thanks to Thee with joy, do now beseech Thee for the sins of my mother. Hearken unto me, I entreat Thee, by the Medicine of our wounds, who hung upon the tree, and now *sitting at Thy right hand maketh intercession to Thee for us.* I know that she dealt mercifully, and from her heart *forgave her debtors their debts; do Thou also forgive her debts,* whatever she may have contracted in so many years, since the water of salvation. Forgive her, Lord, forgive, I beseech Thee; *enter not into judgment with her. Let Thy mercy be exalted above Thy justice,* since Thy words are true, and *Thou hast promised mercy unto the merciful;* which Thou gavest them to be, *who wilt have mercy on whom Thou wilt have mercy;* and wilt *have compassion on whom Thou hast had compassion.*

And, I believe, Thou hast already done what I ask; but *accept, O Lord, the free-will offerings of my mouth.* For she, the day of her dissolution now at hand, took no thought to have her body sumptuously wound up, or embalmed with spices; nor desired she a choice monument, or to be buried in her own land. These things she enjoined us not; but desired only to have her name commemorated at Thy Altar, which she had served without intermission of one day: whence she knew that holy sacrifice to be dispensed, by which the *handwriting that was against us, is blotted out;* through which the enemy was triumphed over, who summing up our offences, and seeking what to lay to our charge, *found nothing in Him,* in whom we conquer. Who shall restore to Him the innocent blood? Who repay Him the price wherewith He bought us, and so take us from Him? Unto the Sacrament of which our ransom, Thy handmaid bound her soul by the bond of faith. Let none sever her from Thy protection: let neither *the lion nor the dragon* interpose himself by force or fraud. For she will not answer that she owes nothing, lest she be convicted and seized by the crafty accuser: but she will answer, that *her sins are forgiven* her by Him, to whom none can repay that price, which He, who owed nothing, paid for us.

May she rest then in peace with the husband, before and after whom she had never any; whom she obeyed, *with patience bringing forth fruit* unto Thee, that she might win him also unto Thee. And inspire, O Lord my God, inspire Thy servants my brethren, Thy sons my masters, whom with voice, and heart, and pen I serve, that so many as shall read these confessions, may at Thy Altar remember Monnica Thy handmaid, with Patricius, her sometime husband, by whose bodies Thou broughtest me into this life, how, I know not. May they with devout affection remember my parents in this transitory light, my brethren under Thee our Father in our Catholic Mother, and my fellow-citizens in that eternal Jerusalem, which Thy pilgrim people sigheth after from their Exodus, even unto their return thither. That so, my mother's last request of me, may through my confessions, more than through my prayers, be, through the prayers of many, more abundantly fulfilled to her.

THE BOOK OF MEMORY

In this book Augustine inquires by what faculty we can know God at all, whence he enlarges on the mysterious character of the memory, wherein God, being made known, dwells, but which could not discover Him.

LET me know Thee, O Lord, who knowest me: *let me know Thee, as I am known.* Power of my soul, enter into it, and fit it for Thee, that Thou mayest have and hold it *without spot or wrinkle.* This is my hope, *therefore do I speak*; and in this hope do I rejoice, when I rejoice healthfully. Other things of this life are the less to be sorrowed for, the more they are sorrowed for; and the more to be sorrowed for, the less men sorrow for them. For behold, Thou *lovest the truth,* and *he that doth it, cometh to the light.* This would I do in my heart before Thee in confession: and in my writing, before many witnesses.

Do Thou, my inmost Physician, make plain unto me, what fruit I may reap by doing it. For the confessions of my past sins, which Thou hast *forgiven and covered,* that Thou mightest bless me in Thee, changing my soul by Faith and Thy Sacrament, when read and heard, stir up the heart, that it sleep not in despair and say, " I cannot," but awake in the love of Thy mercy and the sweetness of Thy grace, whereby, whoso *is weak, is strong*, when by it he became conscious of his own weakness. And the good delight to hear of the past evils of such as are now freed from them, not because they are evils, but because they have been and are not. With what fruit then, O Lord my God, to whom my conscience daily confesseth, trusting more in the hope of Thy mercy than in her own innocency, with what fruit, I pray, do I by this book, confess to men also in Thy presence, what I now am, not what I have been? For that other fruit I have seen and spoken of. But what I now am, at the very time of making these confessions, divers desire to know, who have or have not known me, who have heard from me or of me; but their ear is not at my heart, where I am, whatever I am. They wish then to hear me confess what I am within; whither neither their eye, nor ear, nor understanding, can reach; they wish it, as ready to believe—but will they know? For charity, whereby they are good, telleth them, that in my confessions I lie not; and she in them, believeth me.

But for what fruit would they hear this? do they desire to joy with me, when they hear how near, by Thy gift, I approach unto Thee? and to pray for me, when they shall hear how much I am held back by my own weight? To such will I discover myself. For it is no mean fruit, O Lord my God, *that by many thanks should be given* to Thee, *on our behalf*, and Thou be by many entreated for us. Let the brotherly mind love in me what Thou teachest is to be loved, and lament in me what Thou teachest is to be lamented. Let a brotherly, not a stranger, mind, not that of the *strange children, whose mouth talketh of vanity, and their right hand is a right hand of iniquity,* but that brotherly mind which when it approveth, rejoiceth for me, and when it disapproveth me, is sorry for me; because whether it approveth or disapproveth, it loveth me. To such will I discover myself: they will breathe freely at my good deeds, sigh for my ill. My good deeds are Thine appointments, and Thy gifts; my evil ones are my offences, and Thy judgments. Let them breathe freely at the one, sigh at the other; and let hymns and weeping go up into Thy sight, out of the hearts of my brethren, Thy *censers.* And do Thou, O Lord, be pleased with the incense of Thy holy temple, *have mercy upon me according to Thy great mercy for Thine own name's sake ;* and no ways forsaking what Thou hast begun, perfect my imperfections.

This is the fruit of my confessions of what I am, not of what I have been, to confess this, not before Thee only, in a secret *exultation with trembling,* and a secret sorrow with hope; but in the ears also of the believing sons of men, sharers of my joy, and partners in my mortality, my fellow-citizens, and fellow-pilgrims, who are gone before, or are to follow on, companions of my way. These are Thy servants, my brethren, whom Thou willest to be Thy sons; my masters whom Thou commandest me to serve, if I would live with Thee, of Thee. But this Thy Word were little, did it only command by speaking, and not go before in performing. This then I do in deed and word, this I do *under Thy wings*; in over-great peril, were not my soul subdued unto Thee under Thy wings, and my infirmity known unto Thee. I am a little one, but my Father ever liveth, and my Guardian is *sufficient for me*. For He is the same who begat me, and defends me: and Thou Thyself art all my good; Thou, Almighty, who art with me, yea, before I am with Thee. To such then whom Thou commandest me to serve will I discover, not what I have been, but what I now am, and what I yet am. *But neither do I judge myself.* Thus therefore I would be heard.

For *Thou, Lord, dost judge me*; because, although *no man knoweth the things of a man, but the spirit of a man which is in him*, yet is there something of man, which neither *the spirit of man that is in him*, itself *knoweth*. But Thou, Lord, knowest all of him, who hast made him. Yet I, though in Thy sight I despise myself, and account myself *dust and ashes*; yet know I something of Thee, which I know not of myself. And truly, *now we see through a glass darkly*, not *face to face* as yet. So long therefore as *I be absent from Thee*, I am more present with myself than with Thee; and yet know I Thee that Thou art in no ways passible; but I, what temptations I can resist, what I cannot, I know

not. And there is hope, because *Thou art faithful,*
who wilt not suffer us to be tempted above that we
are able; but wilt with the temptation also make
a way to escape, that we may be able to bear it. I
will confess then what I know of myself, I will
confess also what I know not of myself. And that
because what I do know of myself, I know by Thy
shining upon me; and what I know not of myself,
so long know I not it, until *my darkness be made*
as the noon-day in Thy countenance.

Not with doubting, but with assured conscious-
ness, do I love Thee, Lord. Thou hast stricken
my heart with Thy word, and I loved Thee. Yea
also *heaven, and earth, and all that therein is,* behold,
on every side they bid me love Thee; nor cease to
say so unto all, *that they may be without excuse.*
But more deeply *wilt Thou have mercy on whom*
Thou wilt have mercy, and wilt have compassion on
whom Thou hast had compassion : else in deaf ears
do the heaven and the earth speak Thy praises.
But what do I love, when I love Thee? not beauty
of bodies, nor the fair harmony of time, nor the
brightness of the light, so gladsome to our eyes, nor
sweet melodies of varied songs, nor the fragrant
smell of flowers, and ointments, and spices, not
manna and honey, not limbs acceptable to embrace-
ments of flesh. None of these I love, when I love
my God; and yet I love a kind of light, and melody,
and fragrance, and meat, and embracement, when
I love my God, the light, melody, fragrance, meat,
embracement of my inner man: where there

shineth unto my soul, what space cannot contain, and there soundeth, what time beareth not away, and there smelleth, what breathing disperseth not, and there tasteth, what eating diminisheth not, and there clingeth, what satiety divorceth not. This is it which I love, when I love my God.

And what is this? I asked the earth, and it answered me, "I am not He"; and whatsoever are in it, confessed the same. I asked the sea and the deeps, and the living creeping things, and they answered, "We are not thy God, seek above us." I asked the moving air; and the whole air with his inhabitants answered, "Anaximenes was deceived, I am not God." I asked the heavens, sun, moon, stars, "Nor (say they) are we the God whom thou seekest." And I replied unto all the things which encompass the door of my flesh: "Ye have told me of my God, that ye are not He; tell me something of Him." And they cried out with a loud voice, "He made us." My questioning them, was my thoughts on them: and their form of beauty gave the answer. And I turned myself unto myself, and said to myself, "Who art thou?" And I answered, "A man." And behold, in me there present themselves to me soul, and body, one without, the other within. By which of these ought I to seek my God? I had sought Him in the body from earth to heaven, so far as I could send messengers, the beams of mine eyes. But the better is the inner, for to it as presiding and judging, all the bodily messengers reported the answers of

heaven and earth, and all things therein, who said,
" We are not God, but He made us." These
things did my inner man know by the ministry of
the outer: I the inner, knew them; I, the mind,
through the senses of my body. I asked the whole
frame of the world about my God; and it answered
me, " I am not He, but He made me."

Is not this corporeal figure apparent to all whose
senses are perfect? why then speaks it not the
same to all? Animals small and great see it, but
they cannot ask it: because no reason is set over
their senses to judge on what they report. But
men can ask, so that *the invisible things of God are
clearly seen, being understood by the things that are
made*; but by love of them, they are made subject
unto them: and subjects cannot judge. Nor yet
do the creatures answer such as ask, unless they
can judge: nor yet do they change their voice (*i.e.*
their appearance), if one man only sees, another
seeing asks, so as to appear one way to this man,
another way to that; but appearing the same way
to both, it is dumb to this, speaks to that; yea
rather it speaks to all; but they only understand
who compare its voice received from without, with
the truth within. For truth saith unto me, " Neither
heaven, nor earth, nor any other body is thy God."
This, their very nature saith to him that seeth
them: " They are a mass; a mass is less in a part
thereof, than in the whole." Now to thee I speak,
O my soul, thou art my better part: for thou
quickenest the mass of my body, giving it life,

which no body can give to a body: but thy God is even unto thee the Life of thy life.

What then do I love, when I love my God? who is He above the head of my soul? By my very soul will I ascend to Him. I will pass beyond that power whereby I am united to my body, and fill its whole frame with life. Nor can I by that power find my God; for so *horse and mule that have no understanding*, might find Him; seeing it is the same power, whereby even their bodies live. But another power there is, not that only whereby I animate, but that too whereby I imbue with sense my flesh, which the Lord hath framed for me: commanding the eye not to hear, and the ear not to see; but the eye, that through it I should see, and the ear, that through it I should hear; and to the other senses severally, what is to each their own peculiar seats and offices; which, being divers, I the one mind, do through them enact. I will pass beyond this power of mine also; for this also have the horse and mule, for they also perceive through the body.

I will pass then beyond this power of my nature also, rising by degrees unto Him who made me. And I come to the fields and spacious palaces of my memory, where are the treasures of innumerable images, brought into it from things of all sorts perceived by the senses. There is stored up, whatsoever besides we think, either by enlarging or diminishing, or any other way varying those things which the sense hath come to; and whatever

else hath been committed and laid up, which for-
getfulness hath not yet swallowed up and buried.
When I enter there, I require what I will to be
brought forth, and something instantly comes;
others must be longer sought after, which are
fetched, as it were, out of some inner receptacle;
others rush out in troops, and while one thing is
desired and required, they start forth, as who should
say, " Is it perchance I ? " These I drive away
with the hand of my heart, from the face of my
remembrance; until what I wished for be unveiled,
and appear in sight, out of its secret place. Other
things come up readily, in unbroken order, as they
are called for; those in front making way for the
following; and as they make way, they are hidden
from sight, ready to come when I will. All which
takes place, when I repeat a thing by heart.

There are all things preserved distinctly and
under general heads, each having entered by its
own avenue: as light, and all colours and forms
of bodies, by the eyes; by the ears all sorts of
sounds; all smells by the avenue of the nostrils;
all tastes by the mouth; and by the sensation of
the whole body, what is hard and soft; hot or cold;
smooth or rugged; heavy or light; either outwardly
or inwardly to the body. All these doth that great
harbour of the memory receive in her numberless
secret and inexpressible windings, to be forth-
coming and brought out at need; each entering
in by his own gate, and there laid up. Nor yet do
the things themselves enter in; only the images

of the things perceived are there in readiness, for thought to recall. Which images, how they are formed, who can tell, though it doth plainly appear by which sense each hath been brought in and stored up? For even while I dwell in darkness and silence, in my memory I can produce colours, if I will, and discern betwixt black and white, and what others I will: nor yet do sounds break in, and disturb the image drawn in by my eyes, which I am reviewing, though they also are there, lying dormant, and laid up, as it were, apart. For these too I call for, and forthwith they appear. And though my tongue be still, and my throat mute, so can I sing as much as I will; nor do these images of colours, which notwithstanding be there, intrude themselves and interrupt, when another store is called for, which flowed in by the ears. So the other things, piled in and up by the other senses, I recall at my pleasure. Yea, I discern the breath of lilies from violets, though smelling nothing; and I prefer honey to sweet wine, smooth before rugged, at the time neither tasting, nor handling, but remembering only.

These things do I within, in that vast court of my memory. For there are present with me, heaven, earth, sea, and whatever I could think on therein, besides what I have forgotten. There also meet I with myself, and recall myself, and when, where, and what I have done, and under what feelings. There be all which I remember, either on my own experience, or others' credit.

Out of the same store do I myself with the past continually combine fresh and fresh likenesses of things, which I have experienced, or, from what I have experienced, have believed: and thence again infer future actions, events and hopes, and all these again I reflect on, as present. " I will do this or that," say I to myself, in that great receptacle of my mind, stored with the images of things so many and so great, " and this or that will follow." " O that this or that might be!" " God avert this or that!" So speak I to myself: and when I speak, the images of all I speak of are present, out of the same treasury of memory; nor would I speak of any thereof, were the images wanting.

Great is the force of memory, excessive great, O my God; a large and boundless chamber! who ever sounded the bottom thereof? yet is this a power of mine, and belongs unto my nature; nor do I myself comprehend all that I am. Therefore is the mind too strait to contain itself. And where should that be, which it containeth not of itself? Is it without it, and not within? how then doth it not comprehend itself? A wonderful admiration surprises me, amazement seizes me upon this. And men go abroad to admire the heights of mountains, the mighty billows of the sea, the broad tides of rivers, the compass of the ocean, and the circuits of the stars, and pass themselves by; nor wonder, that when I spake of all these things, I did not see them with mine eyes, yet could not have spoken of them, unless I then actually saw the mountains, billows, rivers, stars, which I had seen, and that ocean which I believe to be, inwardly in my memory, and that, with the same vast spaces between, as if I saw them abroad. Yet did not I by seeing draw them into myself, when with mine eyes I beheld them; nor are they themselves with me, but their images only. And I know by what sense of the body each was impressed upon me.

Yet not these alone does the unmeasurable capacity of my memory retain. Here also is all, learnt of the liberal sciences and as yet unforgotten; removed as it were to some inner place, which is yet no place: nor are they the images thereof, but the things themselves. For, what is literature, what the art of disputing, how many kinds of questions there be, whatsoever of these I know, in such manner exists in my memory, as that I have not taken in the image, and left out the thing, or that it should have sounded and passed away like a voice fixed on the ear by that impress, whereby it might be recalled, as if it sounded, when it no longer sounded; or as a smell while it passes and evaporates into air affects the sense of smell, whence it conveys into the memory an image of itself, which remembering, we renew; or as meat, which verily in the belly hath now no taste, and yet in the memory still in a manner tasteth; or as anything which the body by touch perceiveth, and which when removed from us, the memory still conceives. For those things are not transmitted into the memory, but their images only are with an admirable swiftness caught up, and stored as it were in wondrous cabinets, and thence wonderfully, by the act of remembering, brought forth.

But now when I hear that there be three kinds of questions, "Whether the thing be? what it is? of what kind it is?" I do indeed hold the images of the sounds of which those words be composed, and that those sounds with a noise passed through the air, and now are not. But the things themselves which are signified by those sounds, I never reached with any sense of my body, nor ever discerned them otherwise than in my mind; yet in my memory have I laid up not their images, but themselves. Which how they entered into me, let them say if they can; for I have gone over all the avenues of my flesh, but cannot find by which they entered. For the eyes say, "If those images were coloured, we reported of them." The ears say, "If they sound, we gave knowledge of them." The nostrils say, "If they smell, they passed by us." The taste says, "Unless they have a savour, ask me not." The touch says, "If it have not size, I handled it not; if I handled it not, I gave no notice of it." Whence and how entered these things into my memory? I know not how. For when I learned them, I gave not credit to another man's mind, but recognised them in mine; and approving them for true, I commended them to it, laying them up as it were, whence I might bring them forth when I willed. In my heart then they were, even before I learned them, but in my memory they were not. Where then? or wherefore, when they were spoken, did I acknowledge them, and said, " So is it, it is true," unless that they were already in the memory, but so thrown back as it were in deeper recesses, that had not the suggestion of another drawn them forth, I had perchance been unable to conceive of them?

Wherefore we find, that to learn these things whereof we imbibe not the images by our senses, but perceive within by themselves, without images, as they are, is nothing else, but by conception to receive, and by marking to take heed that those things which the memory did before contain at random and unarranged, be laid up at hand as it were in that same memory, where before they lay unknown, scattered and neglected, and so readily occur to the mind familiarised to them. And how many things of this kind does my memory bear which have been already found out, and as I said, placed as it were at hand, which we are said to have learned and come to know; which were I for some short space of time to cease to call to mind, they are again so buried, and glide back, as it were, into the deeper recesses, that they must again, as if new, be thought out thence, for other abode they have none: but they must be drawn together again, that they may be known; that is to say, they must as it were be collected together from their dispersion: whence the word " cogitation " is derived.

For *cogo* (collect) and *cogito* (re-collect) have the same relation to each other as *ago* and *agito*, *facio* and *factito*. But the mind hath appropriated to itself this word (cogitation), so that, not what is " collected " anyhow, but what is " re-collected," *i.e.* brought together, in the mind, is properly said to be cogitated, or thought upon.

The memory containeth also reasons and laws innumerable of numbers and dimensions, none of which hath any bodily sense impressed; seeing they have neither colour, nor sound, nor taste, nor smell, nor touch. I have heard the sound of the words whereby when discussed they are denoted: but the sounds are other than the things. For the sounds are other in Greek than in Latin: but the things are neither Greek, nor Latin, nor any other language. I have seen the lines of architects, the very finest, like a spider's thread; but those are still different, they are not the images of those lines, which the eye of flesh showed me: he knoweth them, whosoever, without any conception whatsoever of a body, recognises them within himself. I have perceived also the numbers of the things with which we number all the senses of my body; but those numbers wherewith we number are different, nor are they the images of these, and therefore they indeed are. Let him who seeth them not, deride me for saying these things, and I will pity him, while he derides me.

All these things I remember, and how I learnt them I remember. Many things also most falsely objected against them have I heard, and remember; which though they be false, yet is it not false that I remember them; and I remember also that I have discerned betwixt those truths and these falsehoods objected to them. And I perceive, that the present discerning of these things is different from remembering that I oftentimes discerned them, when I often thought upon them. I both remember then to have often understood these things; and what I now discern and understand, I lay up in my memory, that hereafter I may remember that I understood it now. So then I remember also to have remembered; as, if hereafter I shall call to remembrance, that I have now been able to remember these things, by the force of memory shall I call it to remembrance.

The same memory contains also the affections of my mind, not in the same manner that my mind itself contains them, when it feels them; but far otherwise, according to a power of its own. For without rejoicing I remember myself to have joyed; and without sorrow do I recollect my past sorrow. And that I once feared, I review without fear; and without desire call to mind a past desire. Sometimes, on the contrary, with joy do I remember my fore-past sorrow, and with sorrow, joy. Which is not wonderful, as to the body; for mind is one thing, body another. If I therefore with joy remember some past pain of body, it is not so wonderful. But now seeing this very memory itself is mind (for when we give a thing in charge, to be kept in memory, we say, " See that you keep it in mind "; and when we forget, we say, " It did not come to my mind," and " It slipped out of my mind," calling the memory itself the mind); this being so, how is it, that when with joy I remember my past sorrow, the mind hath joy, the memory hath sorrow; the mind upon the joyfulness which is in it, is joyful, yet the memory upon the sadness which is in it, is not sad? Does the memory perchance not belong to the mind? Who will say so? The memory then is, as it were, the belly of the mind, and joy and sadness, like sweet and bitter food; which, when committed to the memory, are, as it were, passed into the belly, where they may be stowed, but cannot taste. Ridiculous it is to imagine these to be alike; and yet are they not utterly unlike.

But, behold, out of my memory I bring it, when I say there be four perturbations of the mind, desire, joy, fear, sorrow; and whatsoever I can dispute thereon, by dividing each into its subordinate species, and by defining it, in my memory find I what to say, and thence do I bring it: yet am I not disturbed by any of these perturbations, when by calling them to mind, I remember them; yea, and before I recalled and brought them back, they were there; and therefore could they, by recollection, thence be brought. Perchance, then, as meat is by chewing the cud brought up out of the belly, so by recollection these out of the memory. Why then does not the disputer, thus recollecting, taste in the mouth of his musing the sweetness of joy, or the bitterness of sorrow? Is the comparison unlike this, because not in all respects like? For who would willingly speak thereof, if so oft as we name grief or fear, we should be compelled to be sad or fearful? And yet could we not speak of them, did we not find in our memory, not only the sounds of the names according to the images impressed by the senses of the body, but notions of the very things themselves which we never received by any avenue of the body, but which the mind itself perceiving by the experience of its own passions, committed to the memory, or the memory of itself retained, without being committed unto it.

But whether by images or no, who can readily say? Thus, I name a stone, I name the sun, the things themselves not being present to my senses, but their images to my memory. I name a bodily pain, yet it is not present with me, when nothing aches: yet unless its image were present to my memory, I should not know what to say thereof, nor in discoursing discern pain from pleasure. I name bodily health; being sound in body, the thing itself is present with me; yet, unless its image also were present in my memory, I could by no means recall what the sound of this name should signify. Nor would the sick, when health were named, recognise what were spoken, unless the same image were by the force of memory retained, although the thing itself were absent from the body. I name numbers whereby we number; and not their images, but themselves are present in my memory. I name the image of the sun, and that image is present in my memory. For I recall not the image of its image, but the image itself is present to me, calling it to mind. I name memory, and I recognise what I name. And where do I recognise it, but in the memory itself? Is it also present to itself in its image, and not in itself?

*   *   *

Great is the power of memory, a fearful thing, O my God, a deep and boundless manifoldness; and this thing is the mind, and this am I myself. What am I then, O my God? What nature am I? A life various and manifold, and exceeding immense. Behold in the plains, and caves, and caverns of my memory, innumerable and innumerably full of innumerable kinds of things, either through images, as all bodies; or by actual presence, as the arts; or by certain notions or impressions, as the affections of the mind, which, even when the mind doth not feel, the memory retaineth, while yet whatsoever is in the memory is also in the mind —over all these do I run, I fly; I dive on this side and on that, as far as I can, and there is no end. So great is the force of memory, so great the force of life, even in the mortal life of man. What shall I do then, O Thou my true life, my God? I will pass even beyond this power of mine which is called memory: yea, I will pass beyond it, that I may approach unto Thee, O sweet Light. What sayest Thou to me? See, I am mounting through my mind towards Thee who abidest above me. Yea I now will pass beyond this power of mine which is called memory, desirous to arrive at Thee, whence Thou mayest be arrived at; and to cleave unto Thee, whence one may cleave unto Thee. For even beasts and birds have memory; else could they not return to their dens and nests, nor many other things they are used unto: nor indeed could they be used to anything, but by memory. I will pass then beyond memory also, that I may arrive at Him who hath separated me from the four-footed beasts and made me wiser than the fowls of the air—I will pass beyond memory also, and where shall I find Thee, Thou truly good and certain sweetness? And where shall I find Thee? If I find Thee without my memory, then do I not retain Thee in my memory. And how shall I find Thee, if I remember Thee not?

For the woman that had lost her groat, and sought it with a light; unless she had remembered it, she had never found it. For when it was found, whence should she know whether it were the same, unless she remembered it? I remember to have sought and found many a thing; and this I thereby know, that when I was seeking any of them, and was asked, " Is this it? " " Is that it? " so long said I " No," until that were offered me which I sought. Which had I not remembered (whatever it were), though it were offered me, yet should I not find it, because I could not recognise it. And so it ever is, when we seek and find any lost thing. Notwithstanding, when anything is by chance lost from the sight, not from the memory (as any visible body), yet its image is still retained within, and it is sought until it be restored to sight; and when it is found, it is recognised by the image which is within: nor do we say that we have found what was lost, unless we recognise it; nor can we recognise it, unless we remember it. But this was lost to the eyes, but retained in the memory.

But what when the memory itself loses anything, as falls out when we forget and seek that we may recollect? Where in the end do we search, but in the memory itself? and there, if one thing be perchance offered instead of another, we reject it, until what we seek meets us; and when it doth, we say, " This is it "; which we should not unless we recognised it, nor recognise it unless we remembered it. Certainly then we had forgotten it. Or, had the whole not escaped us, was the lost part sought for by the part whereof we had hold; in that the memory felt it did not carry on together all which it was wont, but maimed, as it were, by the curtailment of its ancient habit, demanded the restoration of what it missed? For instance, if we see or think of some one known to us, and having forgotten his name, try to recover it; whatever else occurs, connects itself not therewith, because it was not wont to be thought upon together with him, and therefore is rejected, until that present itself, whereon the knowledge reposes equably as on its wonted object. And whence does that present itself, but out of the memory itself? for even when we recognise it, on being reminded by another, it is thence it comes. For we do not believe it as something new, but, upon recollection, allow what was named to be right. But were it utterly blotted out of the mind, we should not remember it, even when reminded. For we have not as yet utterly forgotten that which we remember ourselves to have forgotten. What then we have utterly forgotten, though lost, we cannot even seek after.

How then do I seek Thee, O Lord? For when I seek Thee, my God, I seek a happy life. *I will seek Thee, that my soul may live.* For my body liveth by my soul; and my soul by Thee. How then do I seek a happy life, seeing I have it not, until I can say, where I ought to say it, " It is enough"? How seek I it? By remembrance, as though I had forgotten it, remembering that I had forgotten it? Or, desiring to learn it as a thing unknown, either never having known, or so forgotten it, as not even to remember that I had forgotten it? Is not a happy life what all will, and no one altogether wills it not? Where have they known it, that they so will it? where seen it, that they so love it? Truly we have it, how, I know not. Yea, there is another way, wherein when one hath it, then is he happy; and there are, who are blessed, in hope. These have it in a lower kind, than they who have it in very deed; yet are they better off than such as are happy neither in deed, nor in hope. Yet even these, had they it not in some sort, would not so will to be happy; which that they do will, is most certain. They have known it then, I know not how, and so have it by some sort of knowledge, what, I know not, and am perplexed whether it be in the memory, which if it be, then we have been happy once; whether all severally, or in that man who first sinned, *in whom* also *we all died*, and from whom we are all born with misery, I now inquire not; but only, whether the happy life be in the memory? For neither should we love it, did we not know it. We hear the name, and we all confess that we desire the thing; for we are not delighted with the mere sound. For when a Greek hears it in Latin, he is not delighted, not knowing what is spoken; but we Latins are delighted, as he would be if he heard it in Greek; because the thing itself is neither Greek nor Latin, which Greeks and Latins, and men of all other tongues, long for so earnestly. Known therefore it is to all, for could they with one voice be asked, " would they be happy? " they would answer without doubt, " they would." And this could not be, unless the thing itself whereof it is the name, were retained in the memory.

But is it so, as one remembers Carthage who hath seen it? No. For a happy life is not seen with the eye, because it is not a body. As we remember numbers then? No. For these, he that hath in his knowledge, seeks not further to attain unto; but a happy life we have in our knowledge, and therefore love it, and yet still desire to attain it, that we may be happy. As we remember eloquence then? No. For although upon hearing this name also, some call to mind the thing, who still are not yet eloquent, and many who desire to be so, whence it appears that it is in their knowledge; yet these have by their bodily senses observed others to be eloquent, and been delighted, and desire to be the like (though indeed they would not be delighted but for some inward knowledge thereof, nor wish to be the like, unless they were thus delighted); whereas a happy life, we do by no bodily sense experience in others. As then we remember joy? Perchance; for my joy I remember, even when sad, as a happy life, when unhappy; nor did I ever with bodily sense see, hear, smell, taste, or touch my joy; but I experienced it in my mind, when I rejoiced; and the knowledge of it clave to my memory, so that I can recall it with disgust sometimes, at others with longing, according to the nature of the things, wherein I remember myself to have joyed. For even from foul things have I been immersed in a sort of joy; which now recalling, I detest and execrate; otherwhiles in good and honest things, which I recall with longing, although perchance no longer present; and therefore with sadness I recall former joy.

Where then and when did I experience my happy life, that I should remember, and love, and long for it? Nor is it I alone, or some few besides, but we all would fain be happy; which, unless by some certain knowledge we knew, we should not with so certain a will desire. But how is this, that if two men be asked whether they would go to the wars, one, perchance, would answer that he would, the other, that he would not; but if they were asked whether they would be happy, both would instantly without any doubting say they would; and for no other reason would the one go to the wars, and the other not, but to be happy. Is it, perchance, that as one looks for his joy in this thing, another in that, all agree in their desire of being happy, as they would (if they were asked) that they wished to have joy, and this joy they call a happy life? Although then one obtains this joy by one means, another by another, all have one end, which they strive to attain, namely, joy. Which being a thing which all must say they have experienced, it is therefore found in the memory, and recognised whenever the name of a happy life is mentioned.

Far be it, Lord, far be it from the heart of Thy servant who here confesseth unto Thee, far be it, that, be the joy what it may, I should therefore think myself happy. For there is a *joy* which is *not* given *to the ungodly*, but to those who love Thee for Thine own sake, whose joy Thou Thyself art. And this is the happy life, to rejoice to Thee, of Thee, for Thee; this is it, and there is no other. For they who think there is another, pursue some other and not the true joy. Yet is not their will turned away from some semblance of joy.

It is not certain then that all wish to be happy, inasmuch as they who wish not to joy in Thee, which is the only happy life, do not truly desire the happy life. Or do all men desire this, but *because the flesh lusteth against the Spirit, and the Spirit against the flesh, that they cannot do what they would,* they fall upon that which they can, and are content therewith; because, what they are not able to do, they do not will so strongly as would suffice to make them able? For I ask any one, had he rather joy in truth, or in falsehood? They will as little hesitate to say, " in the truth," as to say, " that they desire to be happy "; for a happy life is joy in the truth: for this is a joying in Thee, Who art *the Truth,* O God *my light, health of my countenance, my God.* This is the happy life which all desire; this life which alone is happy, all desire; to joy in the truth all desire. I have met with many that would deceive; who would be deceived, no one. Where then did they know this happy life, save where they knew the truth also? For they love it also, since they would not be deceived. And when they love a happy life, which is no other than joying in the truth, then also do they love the truth; which yet they would not love, were there not some notice of it in their memory. Why then joy they not in it? why are they not happy? because they are more strongly taken up with other things which have more power to make them miserable, than that which they so faintly remember to make them happy.[1] For there is yet a little light in men; let them walk, let them *walk, that the darkness overtake them not.*

But why doth " truth generate hatred," and the *Man of Thine*, preaching the truth, become an enemy to them? whereas a happy life is loved, which is nothing else but joying in the truth; unless that truth is in that kind loved, that they who love anything else, would gladly have that which they love to be the truth; and because they would not be deceived, would not be convinced that they are so? Therefore do they hate the truth, for that thing's sake which they love instead of the truth. They love truth when she enlightens, they hate her when she reproves. For since they would not be deceived, and would deceive, they love her when she discovers herself unto them, and hate her when she discovers them. Whence she shall so repay them, that they who would not be made manifest by her, she makes manifest against their will, and yet herself becometh not manifest unto them. Thus, thus, yea thus doth the mind of man, thus blind and sick, foul and ill-favoured, wish to be hidden, but that aught should be hidden from it, it wills not. But the contrary is requited it, that itself should not be hidden from the Truth; but the Truth is hid from it. Yet even thus miserable,

[1] " No wonder that miserable man obtains not what he longs for, *i.e.* a happy life; for that which accompanies it, and without which no one is worthy of it, no one attains it, namely, to live aright, he does not equally will."

it had rather joy in truths than in falsehoods. Happy then will it be, when, no distraction interposing, it shall joy in that only Truth, by whom all things are true.

See what a space I have gone over in my memory seeking Thee, O Lord; and I have not found Thee without it. Nor have I found anything concerning Thee, but what I have kept in memory, ever since I learnt Thee. For since I learnt Thee, I have not forgotten Thee. For where I found Truth, there found I my God, the Truth Itself; which since I learnt, I have not forgotten. Since then I learnt Thee, Thou residest in my memory; and there do I find Thee, when I call Thee to remembrance, and delight in Thee. These be my holy delights, which Thou hast given me in Thy mercy, having regard to my poverty.

But where in my memory residest Thou, O Lord, where residest Thou there? what manner of lodging hast Thou framed for Thee? what manner of sanctuary hast Thou builded for Thee? Thou hast given this honour to my memory, to reside in it; but in what quarter of it Thou residest, that am I considering. For in thinking on Thee, I passed beyond such parts of it as the beasts also have, for I found Thee not there among the images of corporeal things: and I came to those parts to which I committed the affections of my mind, nor found Thee there. And I entered into the very seat of my mind (which it hath in my memory, inasmuch as the mind remembers itself also), neither wert Thou there: for as Thou art not a corporeal image, nor the affection of a living being (as when we rejoice, condole, desire, fear, remember, forget, or the like); so neither art Thou the mind itself; because Thou art the Lord God of the mind; and all these are changed, but Thou remainest unchangeable over all, and yet hast vouchsafed to dwell in my memory, since I learnt Thee. And why seek I now, in what place thereof Thou dwellest, as if there were places therein? Sure I am, that in it Thou dwellest, since I have remembered Thee, ever since I learnt Thee, and there I find Thee, when I call Thee to remembrance.

Where then did I find Thee, that I might learn Thee? For in my memory Thou wert not, before I learnt Thee. Where then did I find Thee, that I might learn Thee, but in Thee above me? Place there is none; *we go backward and forward*, and there is no place. Everywhere, O Truth, dost Thou give audience to all who ask counsel of Thee, and at once answerest all, though on manifold matters they ask Thy counsel. Clearly dost Thou answer, though all do not clearly hear. All consult Thee on what they will, though they hear not always what they will. He is Thy best servant, who looks not so much to hear that from Thee which himself willeth, as rather to will that which from Thee he heareth.

Too late loved I Thee, O Thou Beauty of ancient days, yet ever new! too late I loved Thee!

And behold, Thou wert within, and I abroad, and there I searched for Thee; deformed I, plunging amid those fair forms, which Thou hadst made. Thou wert with me, but I was not with Thee. Things held me far from Thee, which, unless they were in Thee, were not at all. Thou calledst, and shoutedst, and burstest my deafness. Thou flashedst, shonest, and scatteredst my blindness. Thou breathedst odours, and *I drew in breath* and *pant for Thee.* I tasted, and *hunger and thirst.* Thou touchedst me, and I burned for Thy peace.

When I shall with my whole self cleave to Thee, I shall nowhere have sorrow, or labour; and my life shall wholly live, as wholly full of Thee. But now since whom Thou fillest, Thou liftest up, because I am not full of Thee I am a burthen to myself. Lamentable joys strive with joyous sorrows: and on which side is the victory, I know not. Woe is me! Lord, have pity on me. My evil sorrows strive with my good joys; and on which side is the victory, I know not. Woe is me! Lord, have pity on me. Woe is me! lo! I hide not my wounds; Thou art the Physician, I the sick; Thou merciful, I miserable. *Is not the life of man upon earth all trial?* Who wishes for troubles and difficulties? Thou commandest them to be endured, not to be loved. No man loves what he endures, though he love to endure. For though he rejoices that he endures, he had rather there were nothing for him to endure. In adversity I long for prosperity, in prosperity I fear adversity. What middle place is there betwixt these two, where *the life of man is* not *all trial?* Woe to the prosperities of the world, once and again, through fear of adversity, and corruption of joy! Woe to the adversities of the world, once and again, and the third time, from the longing for prosperity, and because adversity itself is a hard thing, and lest it shatter endurance. Is not the *life of man upon earth all trial,* without any interval?

And all my hope is nowhere but in Thy exceeding great mercy. Give what Thou enjoinest, and enjoin what Thou wilt. Thou enjoinest us continency; and *when I knew,* saith one, *that no man can be continent, unless God give it, this also was a part of wisdom to know whose gift she is.* By continency verily, are we bound up and brought back into One, whence we were dissipated into many. For too little doth he love Thee, who loves anything with Thee, which he loveth not for Thee.[1] O love, who ever burnest and never consumest! O charity, my God! kindle me. Thou enjoinest continency: give me what Thou enjoinest, and enjoin what Thou wilt.

[1] " Not that the creature is not to be loved; but if that love be referred to the Creator, then it is not cupidity but love. For it is then cupidity, when the creature is loved for its own sake." " He who would be temperate in this sort of mortal and passing things, has a rule of life established by both Testaments, that he love none of them, think nothing to be desired for its own sake, but use them, as far as may suffice for the needs of this life and its duties, with the moderation of one who useth, not with the affection of one who loveth."

That is a mournful darkness, whereby the abilities within me are hidden from me; so that my mind making inquiry into herself of her own powers, ventures not readily to believe herself; because even what is in it, is mostly hidden, unless experience reveal it.[1] And no one ought to be secure in that life, the whole whereof is called *a trial*, that he who hath been capable, of worse to be made better, may not likewise of better be made worse.

The delights of the ear had at one time firmly entangled me; but Thou didst loosen and free me. Now, in those melodies which Thy words breathe soul into, when sung with a sweet and attuned voice, I do a little repose; yet not so as to be held thereby, but that I can disengage myself when I will. But with the words which are their life and whereby they find admission into me, themselves seek in my affections a place of some estimation, and I can scarcely assign them one suitable. For at one time I seem to myself to give them more honour than is seemly, feeling our minds to be more holily and fervently raised unto a flame of devotion by the holy words themselves when thus sung, than when not; and that the several affections of our spirit, by a sweet variety, have their own proper measures in the voice and singing, by some hidden correspondence wherewith they are stirred up. But this contentment of the flesh, to which the soul must not be given over

[1] " The hidden gifts of God in a man's self are not made known even to himself, except when proved by temptation."

to be enervated, doth oft beguile me, the sense not so waiting upon reason, as patiently to follow her; but having been admitted merely for her sake, it strives even to run before her, and lead her. Thus in these things I unawares sin, but afterwards am aware of it.

At other times, shunning over-anxiously this very deception, I err in too great strictness; and sometimes to that degree, as to wish the whole melody of sweet music which is used to David's Psalter banished from my ears, and the Church's too; and that mode seems to me safer, which I remember to have been often told me of Athanasius Bishop of Alexandria, who made the reader of the psalm utter it with so slight inflection of voice, that it was nearer speaking than singing. Yet again, when I remember the tears I shed at the Psalmody of Thy Church, in the beginning of my recovered faith; and how at this time I am moved, not with the singing, but with the things sung, when they are sung with a clear voice and modulation most suitable, I acknowledge the greater use of this institution. Thus I fluctuate between peril of pleasure, and approved wholesomeness; inclined the rather (though not as pronouncing an irrevocable opinion) to approve the usage of singing in the church; that so by the delight of the ears, the weaker minds may rise to the feeling of devotion. Yet when it befalls me to be more moved with the voice than the words sung, I confess to have sinned penally, and then had rather not hear music. See now my state; weep with me, and weep for me, ye, who so regulate your feelings within, as that good action ensues. For you who do not act, these things touch not you. But Thou, O Lord, my God, hearken; behold, and see, and *have mercy, and heal me*, Thou, in whose presence I have become a problem to myself; and *that is my infirmity*.

There remains the pleasure of these eyes of my flesh, on which to make my confessions in the hearing of the ears of Thy temple, those brotherly and devout ears; and so to conclude the temptations of the *lust of the flesh*, which yet assail me, *groaning earnestly, and desiring to be clothed upon with my house from heaven*. The eyes love fair and varied forms, and bright and soft colours. Let not these occupy my soul; let God rather occupy it, *who made these* things, *very good* indeed, yet is He my good, not they. And these affect me, waking, the whole day, nor is any rest given me from them, as there is from musical, sometimes, in silence, from all voices. For this queen of colours, the light, bathing all which we behold, wherever I am through the day, gliding by me in varied forms, soothes me when engaged on other things, and not observing it. And so strongly doth it entwine itself, that if it be suddenly withdrawn, it is with longing sought for, and if absent long, saddeneth the mind.

To this is added another form of temptation more manifoldly dangerous. For besides that concupiscence of the flesh which consisteth in the delight of all senses and pleasures, wherein its slaves, who *go far from Thee*, waste and *perish*, the soul hath, through the same senses of the body, a certain vain and curious desire, veiled under the title of knowledge and learning, not of delighting in the flesh, but of making experiments through the flesh. The seat whereof being in the appetite of knowledge, and sight being the sense chiefly used for attaining knowledge, it is in Divine language called *The lust of the eyes*. For, to see belongeth properly to the eyes; yet we use this word of the other senses also, when we employ them in seeking knowledge. For we do not say, hark how it flashes, or smell how it glows, or taste how it shines, or feel how it gleams; for all these are said to be seen. And yet we say not only, see how it shineth, which the eyes alone can perceive; but also, see how it soundeth, see how it smelleth, see how it tasteth, see how hard it is. And so the general experience of the senses, as was said, is called *The lust of the eyes*, because the office of seeing, wherein the eyes hold the prerogative, the other senses by way of similitude take to themselves, when they make search after any knowledge.

But by this may more evidently be discerned, wherein pleasure and wherein curiosity is the object of the senses; for pleasure seeketh objects beautiful, fragrant, savoury, soft; but curiosity, for trial's sake, the contrary as well, not for the sake of suffering annoyance, but out of the lust of making trial and knowing them. For what pleasure hath it, to see in a mangled carcase what will make you shudder? and yet if it be lying near, they flock thither, to be made sad, and to turn pale. Even in sleep they are afraid to see it. As if when awake, any one forced them to see it, or any report of its beauty drew them thither! Thus also in the other senses, which it were long to go through. From this disease of curiosity, are all those strange sights exhibited in the theatre. Hence men go on to search out the hidden powers of nature (which is besides our end), which to know profits not, and wherein men desire nothing but to know. Hence also, if with that same end of perverted knowledge magical arts be inquired by. Hence also in religion itself, is God tempted, when signs and wonders are demanded of Him, not desired for any good end, but merely to make trial of.

In this so vast wilderness, full of snares and dangers, behold many of them I have cut off, and thrust out of my heart, as Thou hast given me, O God of my salvation. And yet when dare I say, since so many things of this kind buzz on all sides about our daily life—when dare I say, that nothing of this sort engages my attention, or causes in me an idle interest? True, the theatres do not now carry me away, nor care I to know the courses of the stars, nor did my soul ever consult ghosts departed; all sacrilegious mysteries I detest. From Thee, O Lord my God, to whom I owe humble and single - hearted service, by what artifices and suggestions doth the enemy deal with me to desire some sign! But I beseech thee by our King, and by our pure and holy country, Jerusalem, that as any consenting thereto is far from me, so may it ever be further and further. But when I pray Thee for the salvation of any, my end and intention is far different. Thou givest and wilt give me to *follow Thee* willingly, doing what Thou *wilt*.

Notwithstanding, in how many most petty and contemptible things is our curiosity daily tempted, and how often we give way, who can recount? How often do we begin, as if we were tolerating people telling vain stories, lest we offend the weak; then by degrees we take interest therein! I go not now to the circus to see a dog coursing a hare; but in the field, if passing, that coursing peradventure will distract me even from some weighty thought, and draw me after it: not that I turn aside the body of my beast, yet still incline my mind thither. And unless Thou, having made me see my infirmity, didst speedily admonish me either through the sight itself, by some contemplation to rise towards Thee, or altogether to despise and pass it by, I dully stand fixed therein. What if, when sitting at home, a lizard catching flies, or a spider entangling them rushing into her nets, oft-times takes my attention? Is the thing different, because they are but small creatures? I go on from them to praise Thee, the wonderful Creator and Orderer of all, but this does not first draw my attention. It is one thing to rise quickly, another not to fall.

And of such things is my life full; and my one hope is Thy wonderful great mercy. For when our heart becomes the receptacle of such things, and is overcharged with throngs of this abundant vanity, then are our prayers also thereby often interrupted and distracted, and whilst in Thy presence we direct the voice of our heart to Thine ears, this so great concern is broken off, by the rushing in of I know not what idle thoughts. Shall we then account this also among things of slight concernment, or shall aught bring us back to hope, save Thy complete mercy, since Thou hast begun to change us?

And Thou knowest how far Thou hast already changed me, who first healedst me of the lust of vindicating myself, that so Thou mightest *forgive all* the rest of my *iniquities, and heal all my infirmities, and redeem my life from corruption, and crown me with mercy and pity, and satisfy my desire with good things*: who didst curb my pride with Thy fear, and tame my neck to Thy *yoke*. And now I bear it and it is *light* unto me, because so hast Thou promised, and hast made it; and verily so it was, and I knew it not, when I feared to take it.

But, O Lord, Thou alone Lord without pride, because Thou art the only true Lord, who hast no lord; hath this third kind of temptation also ceased from me, or can it cease through this whole life? To wish, namely, to be feared and loved of men, for no other end, but that we may have a joy therein which is no joy? A miserable life this, and a foul boastfulness! Hence especially it comes, that men do neither purely love, nor fear Thee. And therefore *dost Thou resist the proud, and givest grace to the humble*: yea, Thou thunderest down upon the ambitions of the world, and *the foundations of the mountains tremble*. Because now certain offices of human society make it necessary to be loved and feared of men, the adversary of our true blessedness layeth hard at us, everywhere spreading his snares of "Well done, well done!" that greedily catching at them, we may be taken unawares, and sever our joy from Thy truth, and set it in the deceivingness of men; and be pleased at being loved and feared, not for Thy sake, but in Thy stead: and thus having been made like him, he may have them for his own, not in the bands of charity, but in the bonds of punishment: who purposed to *set his throne in the north*, that dark and chilled they might serve him, pervertedly and crookedly imitating Thee. But we, O Lord, behold we are Thy *little flock*; possess us as Thine, stretch Thy wings over us, and let us fly under them. Be Thou our glory; let us be loved for Thee, and Thy word feared in us. Who would be praised of men, when Thou blamest, will not be defended of men, when Thou judgest; nor delivered, when Thou condemnest. But when— not *the sinner is praised in the desires of his soul,* nor he *blessed who doth ungodlily,* but—a man is praised for some gift which Thou hast given him, and he rejoices more at the praise for himself than that he hath the gift for which he is praised, he also is praised, while Thou dispraisest; and better is he who praised than he who is praised. For the one took pleasure in the gift of God in man; the other was better pleased with the gift of man, than of God.

By these temptations we are assailed daily, O Lord; without ceasing are we assailed. Our daily *furnace* is the tongue of men. And in this way also Thou commandest us continence. Give what Thou enjoinest, and enjoin what Thou wilt. Thou knowest on this matter the groans of my heart, and the floods of mine eyes. For I cannot learn how far I am more cleansed from this plague, and I much fear my *secret sins*, which Thine eyes know, mine do not. For in other kinds of temptations I have some sort of means of examining myself; in this, scarce any. For, in refraining my mind from the pleasures of the flesh, and idle curiosity, I see how much I have attained to, when I do without them; forgoing, or not having them.[1] For then I ask myself how much more or less troublesome it is to me, not to have them? Then, riches, which are desired, that they may serve to

---

[1] " A man who makes progress amid prosperity, by adversity learns what progress he has made. For when he has an abundance of these passing goods, he trusts not in them; but when they are withdrawn, he recognises whether they have not taken hold of him. For generally, when we have them, we think that we love them not; but when they begin to depart, then we discover what sort of persons we are. For on that we set not our heart, when present, which we part from without sorrow."

some one or two or all of the three concupiscences, if the soul cannot discern, whether, when it hath them, it despiseth them, they may be cast aside, that so it may prove itself. But to be without praise, and therein essay our powers, must we live ill, yea so abandonedly and atrociously, that no one should know without detesting us? What greater madness can be said, or thought of? But if praise useth and ought to accompany a good life and good works, we ought as little to forgo its company, as good life itself. Yet I know not, whether I can well or ill be without anything, unless it be absent.

What then do I confess unto Thee in this kind of temptation, O Lord? What, but that I am delighted with praise, but with truth itself more than with praise? For were it proposed to me, whether I would, being frenzied in error on all things, be praised by all men, or being consistent and most settled in the truth be blamed by all, I see which I should choose. Yet fain would I, that the approbation of another should not even increase my joy for any good in me. Yet I own, it doth increase it, and not so only, but dispraise doth diminish it. And when I am troubled at this my misery, an excuse occurs to me, which of what value it is, Thou God knowest, for it leaves me uncertain. For since Thou hast commanded us not continency alone, that is, from what things to refrain our love, but righteousness also, that is, whereon to bestow it, and hast willed us to love not Thee only, but our neighbour also; often, when pleased with intelligent praise, I seem to myself to be pleased with the proficiency or towardliness of my neighbour, or to be grieved for evil in him, when I hear him dispraise either what he understands not, or is good. For sometimes I am grieved at my own praise, either when those things be praised in me, in which I mislike myself, or even lesser and slight goods are more esteemed than they ought. But again how know I whether I am therefore thus affected, because I would not have him who praiseth me differ from me about myself; not as being influenced by concern for him, but because those same good things which please me in myself, please me more when they please another also? For somehow I am not praised when my judgment of myself is not praised; forasmuch as either those things are praised, which displease me; or those more, which please me less. Am I then doubtful of myself in this matter?

Behold, in Thee, O Truth, I see, that I ought not to be moved at my own praises, for my own sake, but for the good of my neighbour.[1] And whether it be so with me, I know not. For herein I know less of myself, than of Thee. I beseech now, O my God, discover to me myself also, that

[1] "For the praise of man ought not to be desired by a well-doer, but to follow him, that they may profit who can imitate also what they praise, not that he should think that he had any advantage, whom they praise."

I may confess unto my brethren, who are to pray
for me, wherein I find myself maimed. Let me
examine myself again more diligently. If in my
praise I am moved with the good of my neighbour,
why am I less moved if another be unjustly dispraised than if it be myself? Why am I more
stung by reproach cast upon myself, than at that
cast upon another, with the same injustice, before
me? Know I not this also? or is it at last that I
deceive myself, and do not the truth before Thee
in my heart and tongue? This madness put far
from me, O Lord, lest mine own mouth be to me
the *sinner's oil to make fat my head*. *I am poor and
needy;* yet best, while in hidden groanings I
displease myself, and seek Thy mercy, until what
is lacking in my defective state be renewed and
perfected, on to that peace which the eye of the
proud knoweth not.

Thus then have I considered the sicknesses of
my sins in that threefold concupiscence, and have
called Thy right hand to my help. For with a
wounded heart have I beheld Thy brightness, and
stricken back I said, " Who can attain thither?
I am cast away from the sight of Thine eyes."
Thou art the Truth who presidest over all, but
I through my covetousness would not indeed
forgo Thee, but would with Thee possess a lie;
as no man would in such wise speak falsely,
as himself to be ignorant of the truth. So
then I lost Thee, because Thou vouchsafest not
to be possessed with a lie.

Whom could I find to reconcile me to Thee? was I to have recourse to angels? by what prayers? by what sacraments? Many endeavouring to return unto Thee, and of themselves unable, have, as I hear, tried this, and fallen into the desire of curious visions, and been accounted worthy to be deluded. For they, being high minded, sought Thee by the pride of learning, swelling out, rather than smiting upon, their breasts, and so by the agreement of their heart, drew unto themselves the *princes of the air*, the fellow-conspirators of their pride, by whom, through magical influences, they were deceived, seeking a mediator, by whom they might be purged, and there was none. For the devil it was, *transforming himself into an angel of light*. And it much enticed proud flesh, that he had no body of flesh. For they were mortal, and sinners; but Thou, Lord, to whom they proudly sought to be reconciled, art immortal, and without sin. But a mediator between God and man must have something like to God, something like to men; lest being in both like to man, he should be far from God: or if in both like to God, too unlike man: and so not be a mediator. That deceitful mediator then, by whom in Thy secret judgments pride deserved to be deluded, hath one thing in common with man, that is sin; another, he would seem to have in common with God; and not being clothed with the mortality of flesh, would vaunt himself to be immortal. But since *the wages of sin is death*, this hath he in common with men, that with them he should be condemned to death.

But the true Mediator, Whom in Thy secret mercy Thou hast showed to the humble, and sentest, that by His example also they might learn that same humility, that *Mediator between God and man, the Man Christ Jesus*, appeared betwixt mortal sinners and the immortal Just One; mortal with men, just with God: that because the wages of righteousness is life and peace, He might by a righteousness conjoined with God, make void that death of sinners, now made righteous, which He willed to have in common with them. Hence He was showed forth to holy men of old; that so they, through faith in His Passion to come, as we through faith of it passed, might be saved. For as Man, He was a Mediator; but as the Word, not in the middle between God and man, because equal to God, and God with God, and together one God.

How hast Thou loved us, good Father, who *sparedst not Thine only Son, but deliveredst Him up for us ungodly*! How hast Thou loved us, for whom, *He that thought it no robbery to be equal with Thee, was made subject even to the death of the cross*, He alone *free among the dead, having power to lay down His life, and power to take it again*: for us to Thee both Victor and Victim, and therefore Victor, because the Victim; for us to Thee Priest and Sacrifice, and therefore Priest because the Sacrifice; making us to Thee, of servants, sons, by being born of Thee, and serving us. Well then is my hope strong in Him, that Thou *wilt heal all my infirmities*, by Him Who *sitteth at Thy right hand and maketh intercession for us*; else should I despair. For many and great are my infirmities, many they are, and great; but Thy medicine is mightier. We might imagine that Thy Word was far from any union with man, and despair of ourselves, unless He had been *made flesh and dwelt among us*.

Affrighted with my sins and the burthen of my misery, I had cast in my heart, and had purposed to *flee to the wilderness*: but Thou forbadest me, and strengthenedst me, saying, *Therefore Christ died for all, that they which live may now no longer live unto themselves, but unto Him that died for them*. See, Lord, I *cast my care upon Thee*, that I may live, and *consider wondrous things out of Thy law*. Thou knowest my unskilfulness, and my infirmities; teach me, and heal me. He Thine only Son, *in Whom are hid all the treasures of wisdom and knowledge*, hath redeemed me with His blood. *Let not the proud speak evil of me;* because I meditate on my ransom, and eat and drink, and communicate it; and *poor*, desired to be *satisfied* from Him, amongst those that *eat and are satisfied, and they shall praise the Lord who seek Him*.

THE HEAVEN AND THE EARTH

"IN the Beginning Thou madest heaven and earth." Moses wrote this, wrote and departed, passed hence from Thee to Thee; nor is he now before me. For if he were, I would hold him and ask him, and beseech him by Thee to open these things unto me, and would lay the ears of my body to the sounds bursting out of his mouth. And should he speak Hebrew, in vain will it strike on my senses, nor would aught of it touch my mind; but if Latin, I should know what he said. But whence should I know, whether he spake truth? Yea, and if I knew this also, should I know it from him? Truly within me, within, in the chamber of my thoughts, Truth, neither Hebrew, nor Greek, nor Latin, nor barbarian, without organs of voice or tongue, or sound of syllables, would say, " It is truth," and I forthwith should say confidently to that man of Thine, " Thou sayest truly." Whereas then I cannot inquire of him, Thee, Thee I beseech, O Truth, full of whom he spake truth, Thee, my God, I beseech, forgive my sins; and Thou, who gavest him Thy servant to speak these things, give to me also to understand them.

Behold, the heavens and the earth are; they proclaim that they were created; for they change and vary. Whereas whatsoever hath not been made, and yet is, hath nothing in it, which before it had not; and this it is, to change and vary. They proclaim also, that they made not themselves: "Therefore we are, because we have been made; we were not therefore, before we were, so as to make ourselves." Now the evidence of the thing is the voice of the speakers. Thou therefore, Lord, madest them; who art beautiful, for they are beautiful; who art good, for they are good; who art, for they are; yet are they not beautiful nor good, nor are they, as Thou their Creator art; compared with whom, they are neither beautiful, nor good, nor are. This we know, thanks be to Thee. And our knowledge, compared with Thy knowledge, is ignorance.

But how didst Thou *make the heaven and the earth?* and what the engine of Thy so mighty fabric? For it was not as a human artificer, forming one body from another, according to the discretion of his mind, which can in some way invest with such a form, as it seeth in itself by its inward eye. And whence should he be able to do this, unless Thou hadst made that mind? and he invests with a form what already existeth, and hath a being, as clay, or stone, or wood, or gold, or the like. And whence should they be, hadst not Thou appointed them? Thou madest the artificer his body, Thou the mind commanding the limbs, Thou the matter whereof he makes anything; Thou the apprehension whereby to take in his art,

and see within what he doth without; Thou the
sense of his body, whereby, as by an interpreter,
he may from mind to matter convey that which
he doth, and report to his mind what is done;
that it within may consult the truth, which pre-
sideth over itself, whether it be well done or no.
All these praise Thee, the Creator of all. But how
dost Thou make them? how, O God, didst Thou
make heaven and earth? Verily, neither in the
heaven, nor in the earth, didst Thou *make heaven
and earth*; nor in the air, or waters, seeing these
also belong to *the heaven and the earth*; nor in the
whole world didst Thou make the whole world;
because there was no place where to make it,
before it was made, that it might be. Nor didst
Thou hold anything in Thy hand, whereof to
make heaven and earth. For whence shouldest
Thou have this, which Thou hadst not made,
thereof to make anything? For what is, but because
Thou art? Therefore *Thou spakest, and they were
made, and in Thy Word Thou madest them.*

But how didst Thou speak? In the way that the
voice came *out of the cloud, saying, This is my
beloved Son?* For that voice passed by and passed
away, began and ended; the syllables sounded and
passed away, the second after the first, the third
after the second, and so forth in order, until the last
after the rest, and silence after the last. Whence
it is abundantly clear and plain that the motion of
a creature expressed it, itself temporal, serving
Thy eternal will. And these Thy words, created

BUSINESS REPLY MAIL

FIRST CLASS MAIL   PERMIT NO. 6448   CHICAGO, IL

POSTAGE WILL BE PAID BY ADDRESSEE

MOODY CORRESPONDENCE SCHOOL

A MINISTRY OF MOODY BIBLE INSTITUTE

820 NORTH LASALLE DRIVE

CHICAGO, ILLINOIS   60610-9975

NO POSTAGE
NECESSARY
IF MAILED
IN THE
UNITED STATES

You Can learn Greek and Hebrew at home

If you've dreamed of learning Greek or Hebrew, but travel, time and cost have held you back, here's your opportunity. You can now study under some of America's leading theologians with Moody Correspondence School's cassette-study guide program. It's ideal for seminary students, pastors, teachers, missionaries . . . anyone interested in adding a deeper dimension to their understanding of God's Word.

Working at your own pace, you'll earn college credit, and discover new meaning in the root words of the Bible's original languages. As you learn at home, your personal Bible study will be enriched. Your Moody instructor will evaluate all your work and offer personal counsel.

for a time, the outward ear reported to the intelligent soul, whose inward ear lay listening to Thy Eternal Word. But she compared these words sounding in time, with that Thy Eternal Word in silence, and said, " It is different, far different. These words are far beneath me, nor are they, because they flee and pass away; but the *Word of* my *Lord abideth* above me *for ever.*" If then in sounding and passing words Thou saidst that *heaven and earth should be made,* and so *madest heaven and earth,* there was a corporeal creature before heaven and earth, by whose motions in time that voice might take his course in time. But there was nought corporeal before *heaven and earth;* or if there were, surely Thou hadst, without such a passing voice, created that, whereof to make this passing voice, by which to say, *Let the heaven and the earth be made.* For whatsoever that were, whereof such a voice were made, unless by Thee it were made, it could not be at all. By what Word then didst Thou speak, that a body might be made, whereby these words again might be made?

Thou callest us then to understand the *Word, God, with* Thee *God,* which is spoken eternally, and by It are all things spoken eternally. For what was spoken was not spoken successively, one thing concluded that the next might be spoken, but all things together and eternally.[1] Else have we

[1] " For in the Eternal, speaking properly, there is neither anything past, as though it had passed away, nor anything future, as though it were not as yet, but whatsoever is, only is."

time and change; and not a true eternity nor true immortality. This I know, O my God, and give thanks. I know, I confess to Thee, O Lord, and with me there knows and blesses Thee, whoso is not unthankful to assured Truth. We know, Lord, we know; since inasmuch as anything is not which was, and is, which was not, so far forth it dieth and ariseth. Nothing then of Thy Word doth give place or replace, because It is truly immortal and eternal. And therefore unto the Word coeternal with Thee Thou dost at once and eternally say all that Thou dost say; and whatever Thou sayest shall be made is made; nor dost Thou make, otherwise than by saying; and yet are not all things made together, or everlasting, which Thou makest by saying.

Why, I beseech Thee, O Lord my God? I see it in a way; but how to express it, I know not, unless it be, that whatsoever begins to be, and leaves off to be, begins then, and leaves off then, when in Thy eternal Reason it is known, that it ought to begin or leave off; in which Reason nothing beginneth or leaveth off. This is Thy Word, which is also " the Beginning, because also It speaketh unto us." Thus in the Gospel He speaketh through the flesh; and this sounded outwardly in the ears of men; that it might be believed and sought inwardly, and found in the eternal Verity; where the *good* and only *Master* teacheth all His disciples. There, Lord, hear I Thy voice speaking unto me; because He speaketh unto us, who teacheth us; but He that teacheth us not, though He speaketh, to us He speaketh not. Who now teacheth us, but the unchangeable Truth? for even when we are admonished through a changeable creature, we are but led to the unchangeable Truth; where we learn truly, *while we stand and hear Him*, and *rejoice greatly because of the Bridegroom's voice*, restoring us to Him, from Whom we are. And therefore the Beginning, because unless It abided, there should not, when we went astray, be whither to return.[1] But when we return from error, it is through knowing that we return; and that we may know, He teacheth us, *because* He is *the Beginning, and speaking unto us.*

In this *Beginning*, O God, *hast Thou made heaven and earth*, in Thy Word, in Thy Son, in Thy Power, in Thy Wisdom, in Thy Truth; wondrously speaking, and wondrously making. Who shall comprehend? Who declare it? What is that which gleams through me, and strikes my heart without hurting it; and I shudder and kindle? I shudder, inasmuch as I am unlike it; I kindle, inasmuch as I am like it. It is Wisdom, Wisdom's self which gleameth through me; severing my cloudiness which yet again mantles over me, fainting from it, through the darkness which for

---

[1] "Whither should the mind return, to become good, but to The Good, when it loves and desires and obtains It? Whence if it turn away again, and become not good, thereby that it doth turn away from the Good, unless that Good whence it turns away abode in Itself, it would not have whither to turn, if it would amend."

my punishment gathers upon me. For *my strength is brought down in need,* so that I cannot support my blessings, till Thou, Lord, who hast been *gracious to all mine iniquities,* shalt *heal all my infirmities.* For *Thou shalt also redeem my life from corruption, and crown me with loving kindness and tender mercies, and shalt satisfy my desire with good things, because my youth shall be renewed like an eagle's.* For *in hope we are saved,* wherefore *we through patience wait for* Thy promises. Let him that is able, hear Thee inwardly discoursing out of Thy oracle: I will boldly cry out, *How wonderful are Thy works, O Lord, in Wisdom hast Thou made them all;* and this *Wisdom* is the *Beginning,* and in that *Beginning* didst Thou *make heaven and earth.*

Lo are they not full of their old leaven, who say to us, "What was God doing before *He made heaven and earth?*" "For if (say they) He were unemployed and wrought not, why does He not also henceforth, and for ever, as He did heretofore? For did any new motion arise in God, and a new will to make a creature, which He had never before made, how then would that be a true eternity, where there ariseth a will, which was not? For the will of God is not a creature, but before the creature; seeing nothing could be created, unless the will of the Creator had preceded. The will of God then belongeth to His very Substance. And if aught have arisen in God's Substance, which before was not, that Substance cannot be truly called eternal. But if the will of God has been from eternity that the creature should be, why was not the creature also from eternity?"

Who speak thus, do not yet understand Thee, O Wisdom of God, Light of souls, understand not yet how the things be made, which by Thee and in Thee are made: yet they strive to comprehend things eternal, whilst their heart fluttereth between the motions of things past and to come, and is still unstable. Who shall hold it, and fix it, that it be settled awhile, and awhile catch the glory of that ever-fixed Eternity, and compare it with the times which are never fixed, and see that it cannot be compared; and that a long time cannot become long, but out of many motions passing by, which cannot be prolonged altogether; but that in the Eternal nothing passeth, but the whole is present; whereas no time is all at once present: and that all time past, is driven on by time to come, and all to come followeth upon the past; and all past and to come, is created, and flows out of that which is ever present? Who shall hold the heart of man, that it may stand still, and see how eternity ever still-standing, neither past nor to come, uttereth the times past and to come? Can my hand do this, or the hand of my mouth by speech bring about a thing so great?

See, I answer him that asketh, " What did God before He *made heaven and earth?*" I answer not as one is said to have done merrily (eluding the pressure of the question), " He was preparing hell (saith he) for priers into mysteries." It is one thing to answer inquiries, another to make sport of inquirers. So I answer not; for rather had I answer, " I know not," what I know not, than so as to raise a laugh at him who asketh deep things and gain praise for one who answereth false things. But I say that Thou, our God, art the Creator of every creature: and if by the name " heaven and earth," every creature be understood; I boldly say, " that before God made heaven and earth, He did not make anything." For if He made, what did He make but a creature? And would I knew whatsoever I desire to know to my profit, as I know that no creature was made, before there was made any creature.

But if any excursive brain rove over the images of forepassed times, and wonder that Thou the God Almighty and All-creating and All-supporting, Maker of heaven and earth, didst for innumerable ages forbear from so great a work, before Thou wouldest make it; let him awake and consider, that he wonders at false conceits. For whence could innumerable ages pass by, which Thou madest not, Thou the Author and Creator of all ages? or what times should there be, which were not made by Thee? or how should they pass by, if they never were? Seeing then Thou art the Creator of all times, if any time was before Thou *madest heaven and earth*, why say they that Thou didst forgo working? For that very time didst Thou make, nor could times pass by, before Thou madest those times. But if before *heaven and earth* there was no time, why is it demanded, what Thou then didst? For there was no "then," when there was no time.

Nor dost Thou by time, precede time: else shouldest Thou not precede all times. But Thou precedest all things past, by the sublimity of an ever-present eternity; and surpassest all future because they are future, and when they come, they shall be past; *but Thou art the Same, and Thy years fail not.* Thy years neither come nor go; whereas ours both come and go, that they all may come. Thy years stand together, because they do stand; nor are departing thrust out by coming years, for they pass not away; but ours shall all be, when they shall no more be. Thy years are one day; and Thy day is not daily, but To-day, seeing Thy To-day gives not place unto to-morrow, for neither doth it replace yesterday. Thy To-day is Eternity;[1] therefore didst Thou beget The Co-eternal, to whom Thou saidst, *This day have I begotten Thee.* Thou hast made all things; and before all times Thou art: neither in any time was time not.

At no time then hadst Thou not made anything, because time itself Thou madest. And no times are coeternal with Thee, because Thou abidest; but if they abode, they should not be times. For what is time? Who can readily and briefly explain

---

[1] " For where the day neither commences with the end of yesterday, nor is ended by the commencement of the morrow, it is ever To-day." Aug. Enchir. 49.

this? Who can even in thought comprehend it, so as to utter a word about it? But what in discourse do we mention more familiarly and knowingly, than time? And, we understand, when we speak of it; we understand also, when we hear it spoken of by another. What then is time? If no one asks me, I know: if I wish to explain it to one that asketh, I know not: yet I say boldly, that I know, that if nothing passed away, time past were not; and if nothing were coming, a time to come were not; and if nothing were, time present were not. Those two times then, past and to come, how are they, seeing the past now is not, and that to come is not yet? But the present, should it always be present, and never pass into time past, verily it should not be time, but eternity. If time present (if it is to be time) only cometh into existence, because it passeth into time past, how can we say that either this is, whose cause of being is, that it shall not be; so, namely, that we cannot truly say that time is, but because it is tending not to be?

And yet we say, "a long time" and "a short time"; still, only of time past or to come. A long time past (for example) we call an hundred years since; and a long time to come, an hundred years hence. But a short time past, we call (suppose) ten days since; and a short time to come, ten days hence. But in what sense is that long or short, which is not? For the past, is not now; and the future, is not yet. Let us not then say, "It is long";

but of the past, " It hath been long"; and of the future, " It will be long." O my Lord, my Light, shall not here also Thy Truth mock at man? For that past time which was long, was it long when it was now past, or when it was yet present? For then might it be long, when there was, what could be long; but when past, it was no longer; wherefore neither could be that long, which was not at all. Let us not then say, " Time past hath been long ": for we shall not find, what hath been long, seeing that since it was past, it is no more; but let us say, " That present time was long"; because, when it was present, it was long. For it had not yet passed away, so as not to be; and therefore there was, what could be long; but after it was past, that ceased also to be long, which ceased to be.

Let us see then, thou soul of man, whether present time can be long: for to thee it is given to feel and to measure length of time. What wilt thou answer me? Are an hundred years, when present, a long time? See first, whether an hundred years can be present. For if the first of these years be now current, it is present, but the other ninety and nine are to come, and therefore are not yet, but if the second year be current, one is now past, another present, the rest to come. And so if we assume any middle year of this hundred to be present, all before it are past; all after it, to come; wherefore an hundred years cannot be present. But see at least whether that one which is now current, itself is present; for if the current month be its first, the rest are to come; if the second, the first is already past, and the rest are not yet. Therefore, neither is the year now current present; and if not present as a whole, then is not the year present. For twelve months are a year; of which whatever be the current month is present; the rest past, or to come. Although neither is that current month present; but one day only; the rest being to come, if it be the first; past, if the last; if any of the middle, then amid past and to come.

See how the present time, which alone we found could be called long, is abridged to the length scarce of one day. But let us examine that also; because neither is one day present as a whole. For it is made up of four-and-twenty hours of night and day: of which, the first hath the rest to come; the last hath them past; and any of the middle hath those before it past, those behind it to come. Yea, that one hour passeth away in flying particles. Whatsoever of it hath flown away, is past; what-soever remaineth, is to come. If an instant of time be conceived, which cannot be divided into the smallest particles of moments, that alone is it, which may be called present. Which yet flies with such speed from future to past, as not to be lengthened out with the least stay. For if it be, it is divided into past and future. The present hath no space. Where then is the time, which we may call long? Is it to come? Of it we do not say, " It is long "; because it is not yet, so as to be long; but we say, " It will be long." When therefore will it be? For if even then, when it is yet to come, it shall not be long (because what can be long, as yet is not), and so it shall then be long, when from future which as yet is not, it shall begin now to be, and have become present, that so there should exist what may be long; then does time present cry out in the words above, that it cannot be long.

THE LIVING SOUL

NOW are all things fair that Thou hast made; but behold, Thyself art unutterably fairer, that madest all; from whom had not Adam fallen, the brackishness of the sea had never flowed out of him, that is, the human race so profoundly curious, and tempestuously swelling, and restlessly tumbling up and down; and then had there been no need of Thy dispensers to work in *many waters*, after a corporeal and sensible manner, mysterious doings and sayings. For such those *moving* and *flying creatures* now seem to me to mean, whereby people initiated and consecrated by corporeal sacraments, should not further profit, unless their soul had a spiritual life, and unless after the word of admission, it looked forwards to perfection.

And hereby, in Thy Word, not the deepness of the sea, but the earth separated from the bitterness of the waters, brings forth, not the *moving* creature *that hath life*, but *the living soul*. For now hath it no more need of baptism, as the heathen have, and as itself had, when it was covered with the waters (for no other *entrance* is there *into the kingdom of heaven*, since Thou hast appointed that this should be the entrance): nor does it seek after wonderfulness of miracles to work belief; for it is not such, that *unless it sees signs and wonders, it will not believe,* now that the faithful *earth* is separated from the waters that were bitter with infidelity; and *tongues are for a sign, not to them that believe, but to them that believe not.* Neither then does that earth which *Thou hast founded upon the waters,* need that *flying kind,* which at Thy word *the waters brought forth.* Send Thou Thy word into it by Thy messengers: for we speak of their working, yet it is Thou that workest in them that they may work out a *living soul* in it. The earth brings it forth, because the earth is the cause that they work this in the soul; as the sea was the cause that they wrought upon the *moving creatures that have life, and the fowls that fly under the firmament of heaven,* of whom the earth hath no need; although it feeds upon that fish which was taken out of the deep, upon that *table* which *Thou hast prepared in the presence* of them that believe. For therefore was He taken out of the deep, that He might feed the dry land; and the *fowl,* though bred in the sea, is yet *multiplied upon the earth.* For of the first preachings of the Evangelists, man's infidelity was the cause; yet are the faithful also exhorted and blessed by them manifoldly, from day to day. But *the living soul* takes his beginning from the *earth*: for it profits only those already among the Faithful, to contain themselves from the love of this world, that so their soul may live unto Thee, which was *dead while it lived in pleasures*; in death-bringing pleasures, Lord, for Thou, Lord, art the life-giving delight of the pure heart.

Now then let Thy ministers work upon *the earth*, —not as upon the waters of infidelity, by preaching and speaking by miracles, and sacraments, and mystic words; wherein ignorance, the mother of admiration, might be intent upon them, out of a reverence towards those secret signs. For such is the entrance unto the Faith for the sons of Adam forgetful of Thee, while *they hide themselves from Thy face*, and become a darksome deep. But—let Thy ministers work now as on the *dry land*, separated from the whirlpools of the great deep: and let them be a pattern unto the Faithful, by living before them, and stirring them up to imitation. For thus do men hear, so as not to hear only, but to do also. *Seek the Lord, and your soul shall live*, that the *earth* may *bring forth the living soul*.

O Lord God, *give peace unto us* (for Thou hast given us all things); the peace of rest, the peace of the Sabbath, which hath no evening. For all this most goodly array of things *very good*, having finished their courses, is to pass away, for in them there was *morning and evening*.

GRATIAS TIBI DOMINE